THE SOLACE

THE SOLACE

Finding Value in Death through Gratitude for Life

Joshua Glasgow

OXFORD
UNIVERSITY PRESS

Oxford University Press is a department of the University of Oxford. It furthers
the University's objective of excellence in research, scholarship, and education
by publishing worldwide. Oxford is a registered trade mark of Oxford University
Press in the UK and certain other countries.

Published in the United States of America by Oxford University Press
198 Madison Avenue, New York, NY 10016, United States of America.

Library of Congress Cataloging-in-Publication Data
Names: Glasgow, Joshua, author.
Title: The solace : finding value in death through gratitude for life / Joshua Glasgow.
Description: New York, NY, United States of America : Oxford University
Press, 2020. | Includes bibliographical references. |
Identifiers: LCCN 2020005849 (print) | LCCN 2020005850 (ebook) |
ISBN 9780190074302 (hb) | ISBN 9780190074326 (epub) | ISBN 9780190074333
Subjects: LCSH: Death. | Consolation. | Gratitude.
Classification: LCC BD444 .G53 2020 (print) | LCC BD444 (ebook) |
DDC 128/.5—dc23
LC record available at https://lccn.loc.gov/2020005849
LC ebook record available at https://lccn.loc.gov/2020005850

9 8 7 6 5 4 3 2 1

Printed by Sheridan Books, Inc., United States of America

For Samantha

CONTENTS

SILVER LININGS

When my mom told us that she had cancer, she also announced that she did not want to find out how much time she had left. She would follow the doctor's treatment recommendations, but other than that she just wanted to live each day as it came, as normally as possible. My brother and I had permission to learn about her prognosis, but she did not want to hear any timetables or odds.

Obviously you want to respect people's wishes in a situation like this. And this was someone with a very specific understanding of what's proper. If others hadn't beaten her to it, she would have invented the line about not saying anything at all if you don't have anything nice to say. When someone like this declares that she would prefer not to talk about her own expiration, you go along.

So I went along. Mom and I learned how to talk about scans and procedures and Erbitux and rashes and exhaustion and hair loss and neuropathy. One of the hard truths about chemotherapy is that its side effects can distract you from the illness itself. We did not discuss death.

I couldn't understand why she did not want to know her odds of living one, two, five, ten more years. I would *need* to know. She insisted that she did not want to change her life to fit some actuarial chart, only to discover that she had overcome the odds and lived longer. I wondered if she just found the prospect of death too unbearable to face. Why do we resist confronting our own endings? Does death have to disturb us that much?

It is easy to understand why the final months, weeks, and days of slowly *dying* can be terrible. We decline and we decay. We endure pain and lose control over our bodies, minds, and lives. We want to avoid those miseries. What I was wondering about was the very last bit, the ultimate passing away itself, the final transition from the forward-marching explosion of life to the static blankness of non-existence. Why is *that* so bad for us? And can we find any comfort in it?

Of course, if death transports you to some sort of after-life where your wildest dreams come true for an infinite amount of time, then that is plenty of comfort. But I was dealing with a more charged question: What if our fate is a fate worse than death? What if it is a death with no af-terlife? If this was going to be it for Mom—the end of her consciousness, herself, her entire subjectivity—what silver linings could we grab? On the assumption that the process of dying culminates in our total nonexistence, the question was whether there might be something valuable even in that passage into emptiness.

Now, my mother had enjoyed a pretty good life to that point. She lived comfortably, and her world included a wealth of friendship and positive experiences. Her kids had turned out alright, or at least that is what I hoped. But her diagnosis shoved a different problem in our faces: whether we could find any comfort in the fact that she would die—in that fact and that fact alone. Is there something that the religious and the nonreligious have in common, something about the human condition as we know it, such that our cessation itself might have traces of goodness? Can there be a rational source of strength to help our loved ones steel their spines when the doctor says *tumor*? What I wondered is, if Mom and I ever got to have the conversation that she was avoiding, was there something reassuring that I could say to her about passing away? Is there some path that can guide us to solace in the very end of our being?

Nothingness

2 | EPICURUS' DILEMMA

Epicurus tried to chart one route to comfort in the face of death. Death, he famously wrote, "is nothing to us, since so long as we exist, death is not with us; but when death comes, then we do not exist. It does not then concern either the living or the dead, since for the former it is not, and the latter are no more."[1]

Nonexistent people are not living in some foreign land. They have not escaped the material realm for better real estate, a spectral slice of heaven tucked invisible somewhere in the clouds. The nonexistent have not been reincarnated as pink fairy armadillos, platypuses, or spiny lumpsuckers. Nonexistent people do not exist. So sticking with the assumption that being dead amounts to not existing after having existed, Epicurus thinks that our question has an easy answer: because you will not be there for your own nonexistence, your nonexistence cannot be bad for you. In fact, from this perspective the pressing question becomes why we make such a big deal out of the whole thing. How could being dead be bad for us, if in nonexistence there *is no* us? This is Epicurus' consolation.

Now, I wanted to tell my mom something that would take some of the sting out of dying. I wanted to be able to offer her some solace if we were ever going to talk about death. I wanted to find some positive value somewhere in this mess. I did *not* want to invalidate the presumption behind her predicament, the piece of commonsense that death is bad. From that angle, Epicurus asks us to take a step too far in claiming that our own deaths are not worth worrying about. I tried to imagine one day talking to Mom about Epicurus' views. Go ahead, you try it: picture yourself sitting in a hospital, telling a dying loved one not to worry, because their fear of their own looming death is completely irrational.

Exactly.

And anyway, there is good reason to be unconvinced by Epicurus' argument: even if the dead don't exist, death still deprives many of us of more good experiences, and it is bad to be deprived of something good.[2] If I die in the next few years, I won't get to see my daughter become an adult. That sounds pretty bad to me, even if I won't be there to experience the loss.

This take on death's badness, the "deprivation account," does not say that death is bad because we can experience pain or other forms of suffering while we are nonexistent. If that's all Epicurus wanted us to remember, then there is no disputing that. Those who find themselves worried that nonexistence will be lonely or unpleasant can remember that if there is no *you* there, then those worries are misplaced. Still, though, death can be bad for us insofar as it takes away a future life that would have been good on balance. When this is what we lose, death is comparatively bad for us: if I die tomorrow, my overall life will in all likelihood be worse for me than it would have been had I made it another few decades.

There is something remarkable about this back-and-forth. Epicurus insists that being dead—being in a state of nonexistence—means that there is no you, in which case nothing, bad or good, can happen to you. This so-called "problem of the subject" is underwritten by Epicurus' dilemma: either we exist or we do not, and harms can befall us only if we exist, while we are nonexistent only if we do not exist.[3] I have some sympathy for this analysis of being dead. But the deprivationists are clearly right, too: death does deprive us of important goods. So is there some way of reconciling these two positions? And can a picture that fits both of them also deliver something like the solace I wanted to find?

3 | PASSING AWAY

To both find some solace in death and make sense of death being a bad deprivation, while simultaneously conceding that being in a state of nonexistence is not bad for the person who has died, let's zero in on what happens to us in *becoming* dead.[1] Again, I'm not referring to all of the unhappy things that can happen to us as life slowly winds down—the pains, the sufferings, and the indignities that come with dying. Instead, focus on the very last transition that we go through: the conversion from existence to non-existence. This focus can capture what we worry about in death's deprivation and allow us to also accept (if only for the sake of argument) that nothing bad happens to us once we *are* dead. And ultimately we will see that it also holds the key to finding a source of solace.

Now, "becoming dead" is an awkward turn of phrase, so I'll instead use our gentle expression, "passing away." As I use it here, "passing away" refers to the immediate transition from existing to an enduring state of not existing—the bridge from life to death. Passing away, rather than being in a steady state of non-existence, is what rips away the subjectivity that makes possible the good in our lives. So if the goal is to capture the deprivations of death, then what we seem to care about specifically is passing away. Passing away is the great depriver.

If we say that passing away, as opposed to being nonexistent, is bad for us, the first thing we get is a direct solution to the problem of the subject. The short version—we'll explore this more later—is that in contrast to the state of *being* dead, the subject must still be there for the transition of *becoming* dead. After all, if passing away happened once the subject was already nonexistent, then she would *already* have passed away, which is impossible: you can't pass away before you pass away. So the subject must still exist while passing away. And that means that even if Epicurus is right that we cannot be harmed once we have become nonexistent, we still might be harmed by our own passing away.[2]

A second enduring puzzle about death is how to answer a timing question: *When* is death bad for the one who dies? If Epicurus is right that death can't be bad for us when we are still alive (because we aren't dead yet), and if death can't be bad for us when we are dead (because by then we do not exist), then it looks like there is no time at which death is bad for us. That would be weird, to say the least.

By claiming that passing away rather than being dead is what harms us, not only do we defuse the problem of the subject, we also have a straightforward answer to the timing question: passing away harms us at the very instant we pass away.[3] That "concurrentist" theory—the idea that the harm of death is concurrent with the event of passing away—is so direct that it may sound painfully obvious: death harms us when we die. But the concurrentist claim is unpopular with people who work on these questions for a living.

Critics point out that when something good is taken away from us, the *harm* normally happens well after the moment when we are *deprived*. For example, if my guitar is accidentally destroyed in a campfire, the next day I might think to myself: I could be playing some music now, but I can't, because my guitar is gone. *That* is when it is bad for me that I have lost my guitar—long after the accident deprived me of my guitar. Or think about missing a flight. Jens Johansson points out that it seems like I'm not worse off at the moment that the plane takes off without me, the moment my deprivation is caused. Instead, I'm worse off the next day, when I could be seeing the sights but I'm not. And like these other harmful deprivations, the regrettable deprivations of death—missing your daughter become an adult and all of life's other good stuff—also don't happen until *after* we die. All this makes it look like the harm of the deprivation is not simultaneous with the cause of the deprivation. Or so says the usual objection to concurrentism, anyway.[4]

(I might endure a harm when I first realize that I am probably going to miss my flight by experiencing the bad state of mental *anguish*. This, though, is different than the harms that we suffer by missing a vacation, for even an easygoing person who experiences no anguish is harmed by missing the trip. Similarly, it's not enough to point out that death is bad for us because it causes us to worry while we are still alive: that doesn't answer our question of why that worry is well-founded—why passing away is bad for us, whether or not we feel anxiety when we see it coming.)

I agree that cases like the missed flight and the destroyed guitar show that we are normally harmed by deprivations long after the deprivation was caused. But this truth is incomplete, for we also suffer a separate harm at the very moment we are deprived of a good, even if that good isn't scheduled to be delivered until much later. This second, immediate thing we lose is the *opportunity* to enjoy that good.

Good opportunities are themselves good for us. We hate to waste time not because we obsess over time itself, but because time has its own value as a perishable opportunity to do something valuable. And Amartya Sen offers a powerful consideration to show that opportunity has value unto itself: we worry about the person who is hungry because she is too poor to afford food in a different way than we might worry about a rich person who is hungry because she chooses to fast.[5] Though both people are hungry, only the rich one enjoys the opportunity to end her hunger, a benefit that the poor person is missing. Opportunities for goods have value all their own, which means that losing them is bad for us.

When my guitar is incinerated, I am instantly deprived of any chance to play that guitar in the future. That is bad for me even before the next time I actually want to play it. And when I am too late to catch my scheduled flight, I am harmed by losing the opportunity to enjoy the full vacation. Standard deprivations are twice bad for us: concurrently, in depriving us of valuable opportunities to enjoy goods in the future, and then subsequently, when we actually fail to enjoy those goods.

This double counting might sound suspicious, but it can be found in a wide variety of run-of-the-mill experiences. You didn't know that your favorite musician would be playing in town next week. When you discover that tickets have sold out, you regret the missed opportunity immediately—to lose that opportunity is bad for you *right now*—and then you are disappointed again the following weekend when you're not at the show. Or say that you are living paycheck to paycheck, and you come down with an illness that prevents you from working. You will be harmed next week, when being unable to pay the rent will force you and your kids to live in the car. But you are also harmed when the opportunity for housing slips through your fingers. Or imagine that your lover breaks things off with you, and you regret, "Now we'll never get to start a family together." If you don't get over it, you'll be sad later, when you are not raising children together. But you will also be sad *right now*, in the moment of deprivation, for having lost the *opportunity* to have a family with your one true love.

Or finally, to adapt a case from Fred Feldman, consider a student whose university application does not get considered because a freak storm momentarily zaps the electrical grid right when she clicks "submit."[6] When would it make sense for her to regret this lost opportunity? It might be later, during what should have been her first year at the university: "I could be doing amazing things right now," she might grumble, "rather than sitting around this dead-end place." But it also makes sense for her to feel harmed at the very moment she discovers that her application did not go through in time to meet the deadline. Whether or not she would have actually gotten into the university, a precious opportunity has already slipped through her fingers. That—the opportunity to have good things in our lives—is itself a good on top of those good things that come via our opportunities.

This is how we can say that death harmfully deprives us right when we pass away: that event is when we undergo one of the two harms of deprivation, the loss of valuable opportunities. When I pass away, I will be deprived of the opportunity to enjoy any future goods, including especially the good of subjectivity, the good of life itself. Passing away robs us of *access* to goods. And it does so instantaneously. That particular harm is concurrent with the cause of the deprivation.

Of course, this is only one of the two harms that we suffer in standard deprivations. In passing away we lose the opportunities for good things to happen to us, which is bad for us. But we aren't necessarily harmed again years later when good things happen without us. (Though that could be true, too, for reasons that go beyond the logic of concurrentism.) If I die before my daughter reaches adulthood, concurrentism allows us to say that I am robbed of the opportunity to see her become an adult, but not that I am also harmed later, when I'm long gone and she actually becomes an adult. So you might wonder whether our view captures enough harm. Do we miss something crucial by capturing only the concurrent harms? Aren't we neglecting all the downstream harms that we also suffer in typical deprivations, way *after* the opportunity has been lost? When my guitar is destroyed I lose not only the opportunity to play the guitar, but also, tomorrow, the guitar playing itself.

Our lives benefit us insofar as they are bundles of opportunities for goods. Obviously our lives are also bad for us insofar as they are bundles of opportunities for bad things to happen. Life ain't perfect. But for those of us who enjoy opportunities for goods—which is not everyone—those opportunities have value for us. There is no good we can receive without first having the opportunity to receive it, and the agency we value is exercised at the intersection where desire meets possibility.[7] That field of opportunity, platformed on our existence, is what we are deprived of at the very moment we pass away. When you lose the chance to raise a family with the person you love, you might take some comfort in the fact that there are other fish in the sea.

You don't have to wait for one of those fish to become your next love; the possibility alone has enough value to provide some comfort. But when you die, the sea of possibility rolls on without you. This is why, even if passing away "only" compromises opportunities, it is still arguably the worst deprivation we experience. In it we lose every good possibility for us. This is deprivation enough.

4 | INCOMPARABLE

Following in Epicurus' tradition, the ancient Roman philosopher Lucretius wondered why we lament the years we will lose after our lives end but not the years before we were born. This asymmetry in our attitudes gives rise to the third of our three puzzles: Shouldn't our attitudes toward our nonexistence be the same regardless of whether that nonexistence happens before or after our existence? The Epicurean answer is consistently carefree: since we do not worry about pre-natal nonexistence, we shouldn't worry about post-mortem nonexistence, either. Maybe that can be a source of solace.[1]

(I am sliding here between the time of birth and the start of our existence. Technically it's the latter, pre-*vital* rather than pre-*natal* stage that matters. When I talk of our *creation*, that is what I refer to—the beginning of our existence as creatures with lives worth valuing. I'll stay neutral on when we get created in this sense. It might be when we are born, it might be at conception, it might be at some point in between, or it might be when we taste our first sip of beer. I don't know.)

Some say that it is actually rational to regret our pre-vital nonexistence, or to wish we were created earlier, or to want additional well-being in our lives regardless of whether it comes in the form of extra early years or extra late years.[2] But even if these reactions are right, that doesn't solve the entire problem. Just speaking for myself, at least, even if I wish I were created earlier, I still do not get *as* down about my past nonexistence as I do about the prospect of not existing after this life that I am living. Is there any good reason for feeling that way?

One explanation of our asymmetrical attitudes flows straight from the story we are exploring about passing away being bad for us. We can just grant (if only for the sake of argument) that our attitudes toward being nonexistent should be the same regardless of whether that nonexistence is located before or after our lives. For this is a judgment about *being* nonexistent, not about *becoming* nonexistent. When it comes to becoming nonexistent, to passing away, our attitudes are asymmetrical for a straightforward reason: there is nothing to compare to passing away, nothing to be symmetrical or asymmetrical with. This is true in two senses.

First, the closest analogy to becoming nonexistent is the other bookend event of life, *becoming existent*. Some have made their stand here, pointing out that from the perspective of what's good and bad for us, becoming existent and becoming nonexistent are obviously different. Put in our language of opportunity, one of the bookends gives us life's opportunities, while the other tears them away.[3]

Second, even leaving aside their good and bad aspects, being created and being extinguished aren't identical processes in the way that the state of post-mortem nonexistence is intrinsically identical to the state of pre-vital nonexistence—in the way that both are states of nonexistence. As transitions rather than states, being created and being extinguished are different phenomena. To have something at the front of life that could be compared to passing away at the end of life, there would have to be some event at our creation where we go out of existence. That is impossible. At the event where we begin, we cannot simultaneously end. Passing away simply has no equal to which it might be compared. That is why passing away is regrettable in a way that does not apply to coming into existence.[4]

5 | SOLUTIONS, SOLUTIONS

So it looks like a plausible story of how death harms us is that it deprives us. If we take this to mean that *being* dead is a harmful deprivation, then we will struggle with the asymmetry, timing, and subject questions. But these puzzles are solved with the idea that *passing away* is what is bad for us. And, because passing away instantly and uniquely deprives us of all of our good opportunities, this captures everything we want to say about death being bad for us, without committing us to some more extravagant theoretical possibilities, such as the ideas that we might be harmed after we no longer exist or in a timeless manner. Maybe Epicurus is right that we shouldn't fear being in a state of non-existence, but it still makes perfect sense to be apprehensive about the losses that we will suffer when we pass away.

So if my mom and I were ever going to have the conversation about death, I would not have to invalidate her fear of her own death by portraying that fear as totally irrational.

We are right to think that death is bad for us. Passing away repossesses all of life's opportunities right when we expire.

But that just trades one set of problems for another. I wanted to be there for my mother as she faced down cancer. I knew that I could step up with the most obvious needs. I could offer love and empathy, be by her side for medical procedures, help out around the house. But I wanted something more. I wanted a way to deliver some cognitive comfort, if we were ever going to have the death conversation. I wanted to be able to say something reassuring about passing away, something that would rationally highlight a positive aspect of the deprivation that was lurking in the shadows of her cancer. And that kind of solace can hardly be found by figuring out how passing away is bad for us. Maybe I wouldn't have to invalidate what I was starting to suspect was my mom's gripping fear of death. But this wouldn't help me reassure her, either.

One of the nice things about many religions is that they offer such an easy solution to this problem. They can allow that passing away deprives us of the wonderful things in this life. They can acknowledge our emotional resistance to death. But they can also promise another, better plane of existence after that. These religions don't have to deny the badness of death. Instead their solace is a counterweight to it, something like heaven, or reincarnation, or enlightenment—in any case another crack at the good (after)life.

On our working assumption that there is no afterlife, these comforts are unavailable to us. That appears to leave us with only two choices. On the one hand, we can call on Epicurus to reason away our fear of being dead: you won't be around for it, so don't worry about it. But if this is all we can say, then our aversion to passing away becomes nonsensical, and we ignore the fact that slipping into nothingness is actually bad for us. On the other hand, we can certify our fear of death by recognizing the awful deprivations that passing away imposes upon us. But if that is all we can say, then we are left with no solace at all.

Out of the frying pan and into the abyss.

So let's reset. Assuming for the sake of argument that we won't exist in some other form after this life expires, and having established that we are harmed by death's deprivations, the goal is nonetheless to find some positive value in passing away. We can accept that death's badness outweighs any goodness it might have. (For that matter, even if passing away were downright good for us, still it could be something to be feared. Samuel Scheffler points out in this connection that moving away from home for the first time may be rewarding and yet still be absolutely terrifying.[1]) The goal is to nevertheless find some positive value in mortality. When I thought about one day having the death conversation with my mom, I didn't want perfection. I just wanted to be able to give her a piece of solace.

That said, as she plunged into the depths of chemo, Mom was still unwilling to talk about death. And I was surprised to discover that part of me was okay with that. It would be an awkward conversation with someone who was firm in finding certain topics, this one especially, unsuitable.

But as her treatment progressed, avoiding the subject was shaping up to be a flawed strategy, too. It was becoming clear that this was not turning into the heroic tale of a feisty and formidable fighter cutting out her cancer and going on to live many more disease-free years. Mom had always had a surplus of vitality, but this was a woman who appeared to be on the descent. In this story, fear was amply reasoned, and sadness waited patiently for you to let your guard down.

Mom's tumors were surgically removed. Chemical treatment continued. Hope swelled, but eventually the scans came back with new spots on them. The cancer had migrated from colon to liver to lung. Stage III had given way to Stage IV, the grimmest stage of all. In this story, the prospect of dying was not going to simply walk away by itself. The conversation became more urgent even as it drifted further away.

Immortality

6 | DEPRIVATION OR RESCUE?

Some claim that when people worry about dying, they normally wish, not to be immortal, but rather to die *later*. This, they say, is the interesting or relevant issue.[1] And those who have escaped a brush with death might cherish the rest of their lives as "borrowed time." But speaking for myself, the most pressing—which is not to say the *only*—drive is to avoid death, without much concern for the time at which it happens. When a loved one's candle starts to flicker, we do not comfort them by saying, "At least you didn't die a few days ago." Even one minute is a deprivation, and in that spirit we might wish for a few more minutes, then a few more days. At the end of those few days, I will probably want a few *more* days. And if I get those extra days, I'll want a few more days again, and again and again. Though this is not exactly identical to wanting to be immortal, Thomas Nagel points out that satisfying repeated desires to extend life might add up to immortality.[2]

If death is bad no matter when it happens, then there is a sense in which it is the same kind of bad for everyone.[3] To be sure, passing away is *worse* for the 20-year-old than the 80-year-old, since the younger person is deprived of more than the 80-year-old is. But at the same time, dying at any age can deprive us of a vast field of valuable opportunities. This is how a certain generic badness in passing away is common to dying old and dying young. It is that common element that makes all death seem premature.

But what about those who endure terribly painful or debilitating diseases, unbearable oppression, or other sources of extreme suffering? Can't death sometimes rescue us from something bad rather than being a deprivation of something good? And since we all will at some point face this fate, why not take solace from the fact that passing away saves us from what will eventually be a terrible life?

When we entertain the possibility of immortality, we are dealing in fantasy about how good things could conceivably be. As long as we are in that space, we are invited to explore the most appealing possibilities. So instead of thinking about our eventual decrepitude, imagine medical science becoming more and more sophisticated as time marches on: we find cures for our diseases, or at least advanced pain management techniques, and maybe even a way to reverse the declines that aging chisels into our cells and our capabilities. We don't know when this will happen.

We don't even know whether the necessary advances are coming at all. It is quite possible that right now we are tumbling toward a dystopia where war is rampant, the earth is barren, and malicious cyborgs farm humans for spare parts. But since we are trying to get a read on what we might wish for when we wish that we didn't have to die, let's imagine a more upbeat future, where resources are abundant, science steadily progresses, and everything is going well, more or less.

Let's also imagine that in this future immortality is a choice. Our fate is not that of Tithonus, the mythical figure who eventually decayed so much that he desired to die. Instead what hope hopes for is something like permanent preservation at the top of our game, with an opt-out clause that can be invoked whenever we like.

If this is humanity's future, what would you say if science could also stall your death for now? In the short term, we would not be able to reverse the other effects of aging. You would suffer. But if you could endure three centuries of pain and deteriorated mental and physical capability, followed by a trillion years of pain-free living with a good deal of bliss tacked on, would you take that deal?

I have no idea what the right answer to this question is. Frances Kamm calls our attention to the awful truth that sometimes it is rational to choose what is worse for us, when what is better for us on the whole is nevertheless unbearable.[4] Still, it is possible that in the longest run, death deprives all of us, even those with painful illnesses, of more of a life that would be on balance good. In this vision of immortality, death ultimately might not be a rescue for *anyone*, including those suffering terribly right now. Of course, even if that is true, death might still seem preferable to immortality in other ways, some of which we explore next.

7 | THE IMPOSSIBLE THING

If we got to stay in our prime forever and never suffered pain or decay in any significant way, we would eventually see and do everything. And then see and do it all again. And then again. Because of this, some worry that immortality would inevitability steer life toward a fathomless pit of profound predictability and debilitating boredom, so much so that we should welcome death. In his dramatization of this predicament, Jorge Luis Borges paints a dark picture: "if we postulate an infinite period of time, with infinite circumstances and changes, the impossible thing is not to compose the *Odyssey*, at least once."[1]

If this was our fate—if we had written the novels and heard the music and seen the sights and loved our loves over and over and over again—then, the worry goes, the world would eventually cease to move us. After not merely a hundred, nor a thousand, nor a billion, nor a trillion years, but a centillion years, after seeing it all so many times that we have memorized every detail, would we lose the kind of desires that keep us going? Would we at some point simply stop—alive, but trapped inside an inevitable and colossal experiential loop, where there is no more reason to do anything and every last impulse is drained from our motivational batteries? Or would we be left with only one temptation, to invoke the opt-out clause and walk through death's door?

John Martin Fischer has pushed back against this line of thinking on the grounds that a life with activities that are diverse enough and repeatable might not be boring or lose its drive.[2] And in addition to the qualities of the activities, the quality of the mind matters, too. Boredom isn't a function of our experiences as much as it is a function of our *perspective* on those experiences. A formulaic film might be tedious when you can anticipate what's coming, but if you are not aware of the formula, it might entertain you. Or imagine traveling to the moon so many times that the experience becomes stale. What would it take to undo that boredom, to block the sense that it is all so routine? Presumably you would have to forget your past experience: memory and anticipation fuel boredom, while uncertainty forestalls it. For this reason others have argued that if our memory, or our ability to anticipate an infinite future, were constrained enough, then we might not find immortality so tedious.[3] That seems especially true if we take Fischer's advice and keep our activities sufficiently diversified. If you were immortal, and if you could only recall one hundred years at a time, and if each hundred-year block were sufficiently dynamic and engaging, would one trillion years really be so boring that your will becomes paralyzed?

Imagine that you can take one of two drugs that will make you immortal. Both will preserve your peak abilities, at whatever stage of life you want. And both will give you a chance, every once in a while, to either take another pill to continue living, or to stop taking the drug and die. The only constraint is that once you take your first dose of your chosen drug, you can't switch to the other one. The first drug will preserve all of your memories, allowing for a powerfully rich life; but it also risks becoming so painfully boring after many millennia that you may be tempted to die. If you take the second drug, you will progressively lose all but your last century's memories; your memory and experience will be more like the lives we live now, but on the upside, you will be eternally free from ennui.

If one vision of immortality, like the one with the second drug, is best, then it is what we should dream of when we dream of being immortal. Immortality could be awful and immobilizing, but if experienced in a certain way, it also might be perpetually refreshing. It might be enough if I desire only to go to the next stage, knowing that after enough stages I may take on a different character or even evolve into a new person. As long as I can value moving to the next phase, such changes might replenish experience in perpetuity.[4] This would not be a single hope for immortality itself. Instead we would hope for lots of life extensions or re-creations that collectively entail a hope for something like an immortal self or an endless chain of linked selves.

But if a perpetual series of re-creations solves one problem with being immortal, it only exposes another. Some suggest that an immortal life would be so different from the lives we now know that many distinctively human values would be lost.[5] For one thing, we might simply prefer to live out our lives as stories that are structured by an ending.[6] And for another, Martha Nussbaum highlights some virtues that change or disappear in the never-ending life: if we don't risk death, then the value of courage diminishes, and along with it the kind of love that requires risking it all; moderation in many of our appetites is no longer essential; justice and generosity in the distribution of resources become less important for creatures that can't die.[7] How would parenting change if you didn't have to consider the possibility of your child losing her life or missing a once-in-a-lifetime opportunity? In fact, if our resources remain as limited as they are now, immortality would require us to stop reproducing altogether, to avoid a pile-up of hungry hordes running the stores dry.[8] And even if resources were infinitely recyclable, still, if we repeat something meaningful—falling in love, having a child, perfecting a piece of music—over and over, wouldn't it lose the kind of meaning that comes from asking, "What if you had just one more week to live"?[9] We set our priorities with an eye on the fact that time is limited. If that urgency goes away, then priorities and rational choice, and the idea of valuing itself, start to get slippery.

What all this adds up to is the worry that immortality might cost us the kind of life we want to preserve when we are wishing we didn't have to die. We would lose the human life, the valued life. Ducking the reaper's scythe might simply remove our very reason for ducking in the first place. Maybe the immortal person's fate is not Homer but Oedipus.

I think that this potential downside of immortality is another false source of solace. If you've loved twenty times, each love does not amount to less love than the person who loves only once. And even if we no longer faced the threat of dying, we could still risk a tremendous amount of what we care about, including relationships, pride, reputations, freedom from pain, and psychological health.[10] What's more, access to what we value is often limited by other temporal boundaries besides death. Living forever does not mean that fleeting opportunities or perishable objects become less fleeting or perishable.[11] Long before she was diagnosed with cancer, we knew that my mom would never get to raise a daughter, as she had once hoped. And you might never get a second chance to ask out that person you briefly met on the subway platform, no matter how long you live. Because these limits and values would persist even if we were immortal, immortality does not deprive us of enough value to offset the value lost in death's deprivations.

A separate concern is that one of life's special aspects would get compromised by immortality. We evaluate our lives by asking, for example, whether we succeeded in our goals or redeemed past mistakes, or whether we lived lives of failure and tragedy. Because these assessments are made by looking at the whole life, Jenann Ismael has argued that our lives need to end if we are to capture this value—if our lives are to have meaning.[12]

There is truth in this: some of life's value attaches to the overall shapes of our lives or other long stretches, rather than just to the separate moments within them.[13] But death is not required for us to capture this value. Even now, as I write these words, and as you read them, we can assess whether our lives *to this point* have been lives of redemption or tragedy. We don't need to die to confront that question. So we have to add this to the list of things that won't help us find solace in death.

8 | CHANGES

Even if we could be immortal and simultaneously hold onto much of what we care about, it is still true that plenty of the meaningful choices we make in our actual lives are made on the canvas of mortality. Falling for a million lovers might not diminish the *love* in each relationship, but it would warp the *significance* of each love in your overall life, as compared to the life with merely a few loves. (Or would it? If you can only remember the last one hundred years, then subjectively an immortal life with millions of lovers might feel the same as a one-hundred-year mortal life. Then again, these two lives still contain loves that arguably have different objective significance.) Rarity can impact meaning and value; being one of millions makes one less special.[1] In these ways the particular *kind* of value-laden lives that we lead now would be closed off if we didn't die, displaced by a life laden with a different kind of value.[2] So maybe this is where we can take some solace in the fact that we will die: while it may be an overstatement to say that the immortal life loses *all* value, still our values are *different* from the immortal's values, and maybe we like our values the way that they are. Losing our kind of valuable life may be a high price to pay for immortality.

What is not clear, though, is whether a life with radically altered values would be a *worse* life. Being able to be more playful and carefree about our relationships may feel liberating. No longer having to moderate all of our bodily appetites could be fantastic. Youth would no longer be wasted on the young if we took the immortality pill that preserves us at the top of our game. Becoming immortal would mean that we lose something, the kind of life-changing poignancy that comes from having one love, or one chance at a certain career, or whatever. But we would also gain something.

It is hard to figure out how to weigh the pros and cons here, and not just because we are talking about a lot of pros and a lot of cons. Part of the problem is that humans are adaptive, and maybe in the switch we would learn to value monotony and repetition—perhaps we would find it meditative or stimulating in some way we cannot in our present state appreciate. And more than not knowing whether we would adapt to immortality, immortality is so alien to the human condition as we know it that it is hard to get a clear picture of how to evaluate it. Getting hold of an immortality pill would present us with what L. A. Paul calls a transformative choice.[3] If we change our lives so fundamentally, we change our value system; and if one set of values governs mortal life while another set of values governs immortal life, then it is hard to find a common set of standards to assess which kind of life would be better for the person living it.

So we can't really imagine what an immortal life would be like, we can't identify what would be good for us if we were immortal, and even if we could do those things, it is not clear that we would be able to compare the two options because each option might need to be evaluated by its own distinctive standards. Reveries of immortality elude rational assessment.

Which takes us back to where we started. Challenging the value of immortality drives us into a tangle of ignorance and incommensurability. It does not leave us confidently reassured that living forever would be unbearable. We need a more secure route to solace. At least, many of us do. We hope for plainer comforts when we confront our mortality—a bankable, comprehendible kind of comfort. That pedestrian kind of solace was what I wanted if my mom and I were ever going to have a conversation about death. It requires us to look somewhere more recognizable than the hazy downsides of eternal life.

But after several months of chemo it started to look like the death conversation I wanted to have with my mom might not happen for a new reason: our relationship was under strain. She had become more agitated. Though I had always known her to be a model of restraint, she started exhibiting new mood swings. An unknown, emerging capacity would sometimes rain down on me and my partner and our daughter.

Of course, it wasn't hard to sympathize. No doubt the chemo didn't help; chemical change can surface as behavioral change. Maybe unresolved issues were finally bubbling up. And surely some of it had to be that despite her best efforts at optimism, Mom was worried that the window was closing. Perhaps her reserves of self-control were running low and a baser form of expression found previously closed channels newly opened. With the pressures building, did she see me as a safe outlet, a son she would love and who would love her back even during a storm?

Whatever the explanation, after enough difficult episodes it became clear that we could all use a break. Doubt stalked this choice, but regular visits gave way to a longer stretch apart. I'd wait to see her next at Christmas and my daughter's fourth birthday.

As the holidays approached, my brother reported that Mom's condition was worsening. By late December I finally saw for myself. She was hollowed out. Her once robust body had deflated into a frail shell that needed a special kind of favoring.

She still did not want to talk about death. And anyway it was not obvious that she was going to die any time soon. In fact, I took it as a sign of confidence that her doctors were recommending minor heart surgery. Hopefully it would make her more comfortable and strengthen her to fight the cancer. So a few days into January I travelled once more to the hospital nestled in outer Portland's hills, to help see her through the procedure. That was the first time Mom ever told me that she was scared.

Relief was our first reaction when she made it through the surgery. Soon after, optimism followed. She had a bounce I hadn't seen in a long time. Before the operation her respiration had been labored, her energy low. A day after, she could breathe with ease. She was more mobile. She was cautiously upbeat. She relaxed.

Sitting by her hospital bed, I stepped toward the conversation we had been avoiding: I thought that maybe if I asked how she felt about me writing about her fight with cancer, we would end up talking about death. She said of course she did not mind me writing about it and gave me a mother's encouragement. When she asked what I would write, I started into the ideas explored in the next part of this book. I didn't get too far before she gently *mmm-hmmm*-ed me and closed her eyes for another rest. The conversation was put on hold, again.

The next day, her weakness came back. To find out if this was just because her body had taken a beating from the surgery, all we could do was wait and see. With my brother and uncle at the hospital to help her through the recovery, and with friends waiting in the wings, I flew home. I had a work trip to Tucson lined up, and then the plan was for me to visit her before spring classes started at my university. Maybe we could talk more about death then. Maybe we had finally found our opening to have the conversation.

As things turned out, I wasn't going to make it to Arizona.

Life

9 | GRATITUDE

Our first two paths did not take us all the way to a solace in death. But I believe there is a promising third route. Its first step is that if our lives are good in a certain sense, then it is fitting to be grateful for or otherwise affirm those good lives. The second is that because life's goodness has a certain quality to it, that goodness spreads to all of life's parts; as a result, our affirmation of life can also latch onto each of those parts, be they good or bad. And the third step is that, because passing away is one part of life, it too borrows some of life's goodness and attracts that affirmation. In the final evaluation, that borrowed goodness must be balanced against death's tremendous deprivations, a balance that will require some kind of affirmation other than gratitude. Ultimately it will turn out to be the thing we've been looking for: solace.

To unpack all of this, start with gratitude. Research suggests that being grateful might make you happier. Even just recording what you are grateful for may help you achieve goals, maintain a higher level of physical fitness, and be more optimistic. *Expressing* gratitude also reinforces prosocial behavior, making us more likely to help one another or even just do our jobs. If you are a restaurant server, writing "Thank you" on the bill can bump up your tips 11 percent—and that is only one of the documented links between gratitude and reciprocation.[1]

So gratitude pays, apparently. But we need to ask the different question of what conditions *justify* gratitude. Most people think that gratitude is a response to something *good*, a reaction to receiving some sort of *benefit*. The question I want to chase, given how death deprives us, is whether there is also some way to be grateful for *bad* things.

On this front, Patrick Boleyn-Fitzgerald points us to gratitude for blessings in disguise.[2] One of his spotlight cases is the Fourteenth Dalai Lama expressing gratitude about his exile from Tibet on the grounds that it led him to interact more with the world and work on his capacity for patience. Securing these good side-effects in an otherwise bad turn of events is at bottom an extraordinary case of a pretty routine phenomenon. A person gets a terminal illness, which is bad; but ultimately it pushes him to reconnect with his estranged brother, which is good. Another person loses a comfortable, lucrative desk job, which is bad; but ultimately it liberates her to pursue her true passion of carving custom canoes, which is good. Sometimes in such cases the good outweighs the bad, but whether or not that happens, we can at least find something to be grateful for in them.[3]

Boleyn-Fitzgerald stresses that when we are grateful for blessings in disguise, we are grateful, not for the illness or the job loss or the exile itself, but instead for its beneficial *results*.[4] The bad elements in these cases are instrumentally good. Because these instrumental goods also have substantial downsides, it may be that if we could get the benefit in question without the bad cause, we would welcome that. If the terminally ill patient could have reconnected with his brother without the disease, that would have been preferable. At the same time, these relationships between good and bad can be tangled, as we explore in detail below: How could the Dalai Lama work on being more patient without having his patience tried? But as a purely hypothetical possibility, we'd prefer to fracture those bonds between good result and bad cause if we could, taking the good fragments and leaving the bad ones behind.

Still, all of this shows that there is a way to be grateful for something bad: instrumentally, it leads to something good, and we find a way to appreciate that. What's more, this kind of appreciation famously makes room for a more complete look at death. Reflecting on our own eventual demise is supposed to help us focus on what is important in our lives, to forget about the little things that don't matter, and to live as fully as we can.

Even here we only value the bad thing instrumentally: valuing death in this way prizes it exclusively for its good side-effects. Unfortunately, these side-effects can be elusive at times. A terrible diagnosis can lead us to re-examine our priorities, but many people seem to have trouble holding onto that perspective while healthy and robust. Compounding the problem, when that diagnosis finally forces us to reflect on what we care about, it can be too late for many of the benefits. When your life orbits around weekly trips to chemotherapy, managing the pain in your extremities, and trying to muster enough energy for a friend to visit, seizing the day means something different than what it meant when everything was going well.

This is why, as the conversation with my mom saw repeated delays, and as the chemo cranked up, this sort of solace was becoming less and less relevant. She wasn't trying to tackle some bucket list. She was usually just trying to get through the day with a minimal discomfort and maybe a couple of laughs. So if we were ever going to have the death conversation, it would need to be about some other kind of value in passing away, besides the fact that it sometimes reminds us to live life to the fullest.

10 | THE 8-TRACK AND THE PEN

Consider a teenager whose parents just bought her her first car. It is not luxurious, and it's not exactly a fun car, either; they prioritized safety instead. And it has some flaws. The paint is faded, the upholstery worn. The stereo is an old 8 track player, with no way for her to stream the music that she likes from her phone. Nevertheless, the parents do give her a perfectly functional car, and given their resources, they had to sacrifice for it, working late, taking extra weekend jobs, not buying each other anniversary or birthday gifts like they usually do.

It's obvious that their daughter should be grateful for the car. Underneath that piece of commonsense lies something further: her gratitude should have a certain character. She should be grateful not only for the qualities she likes—its quirkiness, its reliability, and above all its usefulness. It is also fitting to be grateful for the whole car—right down to that useless old 8-track. To say this is not just to say that she should avoid the *behavior* of complaining about the stereo. It would also be ungrateful if she only thought to herself, "Well, I appreciate the car, but I do *not* appreciate that junky stereo."

Now in saying this, let's not get carried away. The 8-track is useless. But all the same, what's remarkable is that feeling entitled to a better stereo and not being thankful for what she got would manifest a problematic lack of appreciation. The whole car is what the parents gave her, and since it is the fitting object of gratitude, that seems to entail that her gratitude flows all the way through to even its bad parts. Call this *holistic* gratitude: sometimes it is appropriate to be grateful for a whole thing, and in those times we ought to be grateful for even the useless or frustrating or otherwise bad parts of the whole.

The possibility of holistic gratitude reveals something surprising about the value of parts. Gratitude must be a response to some positive value: if an object was *purely* bad, affirming its value would not make sense. If that is right, and if the teenager ought to appreciate even the useless 8-track, then the 8-track must have some positive value despite its uselessness. What I want to suggest is that it gets positive value simply by being part of the valuable car; it sponges value from the whole of which it is part. Goods like the car, goods that demand holistic gratitude, radiate goodness to all their component parts. They are *radiant goods*. The radiant value absorbed by the part explains how we can be grateful for it even when it is useless.

To value the car as a whole, we do not have to value things that come with the car but are not parts of it. If there were a dead skunk in the trunk, it would not absorb the car's radiant value. What gets radiant value are the car's *parts*, not its *contents*. This raises a difficult question: What makes something a part of a whole, rather than a non-part that is contained within the whole? Answering that question is a tricky task, and I won't try to tackle it here. Instead I just claim something more basic: I find it intuitive, and I hope you share the intuition, that the stereo is part of the car while the skunk is not. For our arguments what will be important is that passing away is a part of our lives and that certain other things are not; when the time comes I will try to at least partially justify those more specific claims.[1]

But here's the thing: while holistic gratitude seems apt in the case of the teenager's car, gratitude for the whole thing is not called for in other cases. Call this kind of gratitude *fragmented* gratitude—we can be grateful for just a part of an object or experience, rather than the whole thing. If you enjoy a meal out, for example, you might be grateful for the amazing main dish, but not so grateful for the limp salad. Surely fragmented gratitude is exceedingly ordinary. I haven't tried to add them up, but I'd bet that the vast majority of times that gratitude is called for, it can be fragmented. So why is the teenager's reaction to her gift expected to be different than your reaction to the meal? If she were to quietly complain about the 8-track, why would that seem to show a problematic sense of entitlement that you would not be guilty of if you quietly said to your friend that the salad wasn't very good? What separates the times when holistic gratitude is appropriate from the times when fragmentation is permitted?

One possible answer has to do with the ratio of goods to bads. Getting a car is, for this particular teenager, so life altering that worrying about the stereo would manifest a lack of perspective. But in my view this ratio of goods to bads applies to the teenager for a broader and more fundamental reason: the gift of the car is *meaningful*, where that refers to the significance the gift has for her. Having a car opens up so many possibilities and required so much sacrifice that getting it substantially changes some of the valued stories that are part of the teenager's life: it is part of her transition to adulthood, it will be pivotal in some of her work history and the course of her friendships, and it is a costly expression of her parents' love.

Having dramatic, life-changing power is not the only way of making meaning. Many less far-reaching items that are bad or useless can also attract holistic gratitude. Even though you'll never wear them, you might cherish the ugly sweater your grandmother knits for you or the tacky tie your grandfather gives you, simply because of who gave them to you. Or you might prize the first dollar your small business received. Or maybe it's the cheap, disposable, and now empty pen that you first wrote with, launching your Pulitzer Prize–winning journalism career. These last two keepsakes are cherished not because they were especially life altering, nor because they came from a loved one. You are grateful for them because they are important parts of valuable life projects.[2]

These objects have this sort of narrative value in common: they tie together, in a valued way, with other parts of your life.[3] We have projects and relationships that rightly matter to us and that stretch across the otherwise isolated moments we live through. These endeavors and relationships, and their associated objects, are the building blocks of our lives' treasured stories. And the key elements of our stories—the sweater and the dollar, the 8-track and the pen—are what I'm calling *meaningful*: they have a specific, narratively circumscribed value, which we can either appreciate or fail to appreciate. (We can also over-value them: we might *find* something meaningful that isn't *really* meaningful, such as a deluded person thinking that a random plane flying overhead is part of a conspiracy among the world's superpowers that is responsible for every splinter he has ever gotten.)

Meaning steers our attitudes. If you are a working writer, you might be grateful for that pen even though it will never write again. You might even be grateful for its lack of ink, since that attests to all the writing you did when you started your journey. In a similar way, that first dollar your business earned is worth far more to you than its market value. You wouldn't trade it for a hundred-dollar bill.

So the claim on the table is that meaning is the driver of holistic gratitude. You are holistically grateful for the empty pen, or for the ugly sweater you'll never wear, or for the useless 8-track in the car your parents gave you, because of the role they play in your life's extended projects and relationships. You're not grateful for a good result of these things' bad qualities. Their emptiness, ugliness, and uselessness have no good results, and fragmentation is not the appropriate response. Instead, when these qualities are aspects of wholes that are meaningful to you, you're just grateful for the whole package, good and bad. Where gratitude is holistic in that way, we can appreciate and affirm bad parts or qualities, independently of any instrumental value that they might have, because parts draw positive radiant value from meaningful wholes.

As we will see next, this phenomenon is not limited to mere objects. We love people in these different ways as well.

11 | LOVE

Sometimes we have to muster up effort to tolerate our loved ones' flaws. "I'll put up with your impatience," you say, "because I love you so much." Like the meal with the disappointing salad, toleration reflects fragmented appreciation: we don't like the bad quality, but we know that it is part of the package that is our loved one, so we accept it. In these judgments we are not grateful for the bad quality, and we do not think that it has any goodness to it. By contrast, some other attitudes toward people we love show a lower-stakes version of the Dalai Lama's stance, where we fractionally embrace flaws because those flaws have instrumental value: "It's true, without your terrible sense of humor you never would have shown me what is so great about slapstick!"

And most importantly for our purposes, we sometimes holistically appreciate our loved ones' flaws. Human weaknesses can take on a special value simply because they are bundled up in the people we love. These weaknesses do not stop being flaws. Instead they are flaws that when found in loved ones mean something different than when found in a stranger: in strangers these flaws present themselves *only* as flaws, while in a loved one a flaw can become charming, something we embrace rather than being fractionally tolerated or valued instrumentally.

In a memorable conversation from the movie *Good Will Hunting*, Robin Williams' character, Sean, offers up a piece of wisdom to Will. Will is struggling to sort out his feelings toward a woman he is falling for but also hesitating about. Sean tries to give him some perspective via the following story about the love of his own life:

> My wife ... had all sorts of wonderful idiosyncrasies. You know what? She used to fart in her sleep. Sorry I shared that with you. One night it was so loud it woke the dog up. She woke up and gone like, "Oh was that you?" I'd say, "Yeah." I didn't have the heart to tell her. . . . [S]he's been dead two years and that's the shit I remember. Wonderful stuff, you know, little things like that. Ah, but those are the things I miss the most. The little idiosyncrasies that only I knew about. That's what made her my wife. Oh, and she had the goods on me, too. She knew all my little peccadillos. People call these things imperfections, but they're not—aw, that's the good stuff. And then we get to choose who we let in to our weird little worlds. You're not perfect, sport. And let me save you the suspense. This girl you met, she isn't perfect either. But the question is whether or not you're perfect for each other. That's the whole deal. That's what intimacy is all about.[1]

What would be an undesirable quality in a stranger becomes imbued with a dose of positive value when found in a lover. Such a quality is the good stuff, it is the stuff that we remember—and it is some of what we are grateful for. I am too much of a coward to reveal any of my peccadillos, but my partner has allowed me to share that one of hers is an extraordinarily terrible sense of direction. If you ever go anywhere with her, a good rule of thumb is to go the opposite direction of whatever way she recommends. I find this frustrating. Yet I also find it endearing. It makes me smile.

Our positive valuations of our loved ones' peccadillos are non-instrumental. That terrible sense of direction has no good effect. In fact, it has bad effects for her and for us. Peccadillos also lack contributory value: they don't contribute some value to a more valuable whole. Nor do they constitute the whole (in the way that Aristotle can be read as saying that contemplation is a good that constitutes the good of human well-being). Instead, peccadillos simply *draw* value from the whole, without *adding* any value themselves.

So with loves as much as with cars, we can be grateful for bad qualities because they are parts of a precious package that demands holistic appreciation. Significant gifts, important symbols, mementos, friends and family: due to their role in our life stories they get valued as a bundle, with a goodness that radiates out to their weaknesses and flaws. Because meaningful goods radiate value, affirmations like gratitude can also travel from the whole to the flawed parts.

We find ourselves appreciating them even as we recognize them as flaws.

All that being said, I believe that certain circumstances can demand a change to, or outright cancellation of, holistic gratitude. If Hitler were your son, any radiant positive value that his bad qualities (as an adult) might draw from the parent-child relationship would be completely swamped by their badness. As a result, any affirmation of those bad qualities would be cancelled. And the imbalance of positives and negatives doesn't have to reach Hitler levels for this to happen; in other, less devastating cases where the badness increases, holistic affirmation still gets cancelled. Impatience in a loved one might only be tolerated, rather than holistically affirmed, because the bads can stack up pretty quickly when patience is in short supply. And there is a third possibility we focus on shortly: sometimes holistic gratitude neither endures nor gets cancelled outright, but instead gives way to an affirmation that fits the balance of goods and bads better than gratitude does.

As for passing away, we will need to find a way to pay tribute to the goodness it draws from being a part of life, while also respecting its deprivations. But that's getting ahead of things. For now we just need to register that there is something important in the 8-track and the pen. When it comes to mementos, loved ones, symbols, gifts, and the rest, often the most fitting response to them is holistic gratitude. Their bad qualities get some positive radiant value simply because they are parts of meaningful wholes, and that value can affect how we appreciate them. After gaining clarity on this phenomenon in the next chapter, we can see if life itself radiates positive value in this fashion, helping us find some solace in passing away.

12 | VALUABLE IMPERFECTIONS

Let's register one point of disagreement with *Good Will Hunting*'s Sean: contrary to what he says, our peccadillos *are* imperfections. That is what makes them peccadillos. This is a simple definitional truth: we cannot value an imperfection without it being an imperfection, a quality that is less than ideal and possibly downright bad. Otherwise it would just be another ordinary good. This is confusing—it's a bad quality that is somehow also a good quality. (Maybe this explains why Will, who is otherwise highly perceptive, struggles with the idea of an imperfect love.) Our flaws don't stop being flaws. They are still bad. The concealed and confusing element that Sean tries to uncover for Will is that these flaws can have some goodness in them too, and we can appreciate them, because of our relationships with the people to whom they belong.

So let's distinguish two dimensions of value in valuable imperfections. First, considered independently of any relation to the valuer, they are bad—this, again, is what makes them imperfections. Unpleasant bodily functions, useless pens, ugly sweaters, counter-productive senses of direction: I hope you have agreed with me that, whatever makes something bad or good, these things qualify as bad, considered in a vacuum. However, second, when we factor in the relation to the valuer—it's not just a flaw but a weakness in the love of your life, it's not just an ugly sweater but a gift from Grandma—some positive value seeps in. This is how a plain bad quality can turn into an endearing quirk, a *valuable* imperfection.

G. E. Moore held that the value of a whole can be different than its parts' values added up.[1] So assign some arbitrary values to various elements of the teenager's car, considered in isolation from each other: −2 for the frustrating stereo, +10 for the mobility, −1 for the ugliness, +8 for the fact that the teenager owns it because of her parents' love and sacrifice. If we just add up these values, the whole car has a value of +15. But if we think that the car's value as a whole is also impacted by the way in which these elements combine, the value of the whole might be greater than the sum of the parts' values: +16, maybe, or +21.

In contrast to Moore, I am not saying that the whole car has value greater than the sum of its parts (though that may be true, too). Our point is that the whole contains value that radiates to the part itself, thereby changing the value of the part. In another context Tom Hurka calls this change value *variability*: when a whole's properties are combined with other properties, what can change is their *own* value, not (just?) the value of the whole. This is one way in which you cherish the ugliness in the sweater that Grandma made for you. You wouldn't think of buying that sweater if you just randomly came across it in a thrift shop. But because it comes from Grandma, its ugliness looks different to you than it does to a stranger. Its ugliness converts from crappy to campy. And you will never throw it out.[2]

If a bad quality can be injected with goodness like this, making it eligible for appreciation, does that mean that it becomes good itself? Or does the bad part stay bad overall but become *less* bad, mitigated by some goodness that it absorbs from the whole? From the perspective of value variability, both are possible. But our search for solace is about something specific. I wanted to find some positive value to affirm in the awful fact that we pass away. To get there, we need to sort out how to feel about bad things that might contain some radiant goodness even if they are still bad overall.

It is obvious that the teenager can be grateful for the car, with its overall positive value. But more than that, it looks like she can be grateful for the frustrating stereo, too. This suggests that we can be grateful for something that stays in the negative column, as long as its badness is mitigated by enough radiant goodness to sufficiently counteract the badness. Similarly, assume that because Grandma made the ugly sweater for you, its ugliness only goes from a −5 to a −1. Like certain bodily functions and bad senses of direction, it does not become attractive overall. It stays on the bad side of the ledger. Still, we are and should be grateful for these sorts of bads. They don't stop being bad; they just get laced with positive value, and even when the negative outweighs the positive to a degree, that positivity is enough for them to be affirmed. We can smile at them, love them, cherish them, be grateful for them.

This, at any rate, seems to be the best way to make sense of cases where gratitude latches onto a good patch in a field of badness. Although I see my partner's terrible sense of direction as a lovable foible, I don't think that it is good all things considered. I think it is definitely a bad sense of direction and a quality that she should change, if she could. But I have an affirming attitude toward it all the same. Just as Sean is grateful for his wife's peccadillo. Just as the teenager appreciates the 8-track. We appreciate positive value in the parts of meaningful wholes even as we maintain that what we affirm is on balance bad or useless, or ought to be changed if possible.

So the full picture of how our attitudes connect to radiant value looks like this. When good things are meaningful they can radiate goodness to their bad parts. Sometimes this radiant goodness might be enough to overcome the badness found in a part (or property) of the whole, to move the part into the good column. But in other cases it is not overriding in that way: the bad part stays bad, siphoning positive radiant value that only partially offsets the bad. Yet even in some of these cases, that morsel of goodness can be good enough for affirming attitudes like gratitude. We live in an imperfect world. Thankfully, some of those imperfections are affirmable.

If this is right, then we can be grateful even for bads that produce no good results for us. Meaningful goods stretch the range of things we can affirm, potentially opening up a different way of thinking about death. If life is itself one of those meaningful, radiant goods, and if passing away is a part of life, then we have an avenue to affirm something in passing away.

13 | EXISTENCE

The teenager's car, the writer's pen, the ugly sweater from Granny: these goods radiate value to their parts because they are meaningful to their owners, in the sense that they play important roles in their owners' rightly valued projects and relationships. I claimed that this explains the shape our attitudes take. In some cases it is fitting to be holistically grateful for these goods, grateful for not only their good qualities but their bad ones, too. The teenager chuckles at the useless 8-track, the author fondly cradles her drained pen between thumb and finger, and you store that ugly sweater for safekeeping.

I believe that for most of us, our existence is like this, too: life is a meaningful good, which therefore has radiant value. And because passing away is part of life, passing away itself extracts some of life's radiant goodness. This gives us a reason to feel at least a little bit better about the deprivation that befalls us when we pass away. This can be a source of solace.

The limitation on this solace is that it only applies to people who enjoy valuable lives. By a *valuable* life, I just mean a life worth living for the one whose life it is—a life that has net positive value for that person. So to claim that those with valuable lives can find goodness in death does not speak to those *without* lives worth living. For those whose lives are not worth living, there is not enough goodness in life to make life's parts, including death, any better. Consider a baby who is born with a terrible affliction, who will live two weeks consumed by pain and violent convulsions while stuck in a chamber that prevents him from ever feeling the touch of a loved one, and who then will experience a slow, gruesome death. That child may not have a life worth living—it might be contestable, but let's just assume so for argument's sake—in which case the analysis of life's value that we are exploring won't apply to him. (But death may function for him as a good rescue, not a bad deprivation.)[1]

Most of us, I believe, have lives worth living. We do have problems. Many people have to endure horrible experiences. Nonetheless, this is compatible with living a valuable life—it is overall better for us to have a life with many of these bad experiences than to have died as a young child before those experiences, and it is better to continue living from this point onward than to die today. For those who enjoy lives above that threshold, I maintain that life is meaningful and so has radiant value.

What exactly does it mean to attribute this value to life, specifically? To whatever extent we are tempted to cherish biological life, we should remember Nagel's point that we would not be content to be stuck in a permanent coma.[2] The kind of life we most want is one that includes consciousness. And more than that, life at its most valuable involves active engagement in our pursuits; we do not just want to be receptacles for experience. So since we are focused on having a valuable life, when we here talk about our *life* or our *existence*, let's use it in this value-laden sense, the sense of being a sensitive, conscious creature, engaged in the world, and when things are going well a creature with a robust form of agency. Simply being lucky to live a valuable life in this sense is good for us. It is the basis of all the other good things we get, the platform for our opportunities. It is the thing that we didn't want my mom to lose.

Because the good of existence opens the door to all other goods, there is an easy comparative reason for saying that life is a tremendous benefit. After all, it is because we exist as active experiencers that we can enjoy the pleasures and perceptions and memories and moods that make our lives rich. We can take on extended projects and achieve something. We can improve our communities. We can attain some knowledge of the universe. We can develop the relationships that give our worlds depth. We can play and have fun. Life makes these possibilities possible.

As many have observed, death anxiety stems not merely from the knowledge that when I die I will lose the good experiences of my life. What gives it a uniquely panicky flavor is the further realization that my self, the subject who might lose these experiences, will be extinguished, too. Our subjectivity, our life in the sense that I am using the term, is such a distinctive good that to fully confront its extinction demands new words to capture the distance between normal fear and the fear of death; James Baillie calls it "existential shock."[3]

If life is so important that its threatened loss inspires such a unique reaction, then it would seem to be a radiant good, if anything is. But there is a more principled story about why life has not just tremendous value but radiant value specifically. The meaningfulness that makes radiant goods radiant is a matter of playing the right kind of role in our various stories: meaningful goods are those that positively figure in our ongoing valued projects and relationships. The pen is meaningful for the author, insofar as it kicked off her writing career. The tacky tie that Grandpa gave you was his last gift to you and so an important memento of his love. (The dinner with the limp salad? We are assuming that it is unconnected to any valuable narrative in your life.) Life, too, is meaningful in this way: it bears an originating relationship to everything else of value in our lives. It is the stage on which our valuable projects and relationships play out, the frame for every experience and thought and feeling we ever have. This is the feature that gives rise to existential shock: the only way to contemplate your outlook not existing is to use the very outlook that won't exist.

Subjectivity in this sense is the necessary condition of everything we live through. This includes our rightly valued stories, which means that life has an essential role to play in our positive narratives. Of course, life plays a role in our negative narratives, too. But that does not cancel its work in our positive stories. This role in our valuable narratives makes life not only precious but also meaningful in the relevant sense. It is therefore a radiant good that calls for a holistically affirming attitude.[4]

A potential worry about the claim that life is a meaningful good for which we can be holistically grateful is that life cannot be a *gift* or a *benefit*, because gifts and benefits can only be given to those who already exist, and when we are created we do not yet exist.[5] In response, we could question why the recipient of a gift must exist or even have a determinate future identity in order to be given a gift. You might put aside a family heirloom for your future grandchild long before any grandchild is conceived. Prior to their creation, you have only given it to an undetermined recipient. But still, whomever they turn out to be, it is a benefit to that future child. In any event, a second way to defuse the worry is that even if it were true that the not-yet-existent can't be benefitted—or worse, even if anti-natalists are right that being created actually harms us—that would only mean that *being created* is not a benefit to us. Even if that is true, Jeff McMahan has pointed out that this is compatible with believing that *after* the moment of creation our ongoing life is a benefit to those of us with lives worth living. This last claim, that our *ongoing* existence is a meaningful good for us, rather than the claim that our *creation* was good for us, is what we need on this road to solace. Only those who exist can die. And so if we ought to be holistically grateful for our ongoing lives, then perhaps we can find something to affirm in our lives' bad parts, including the last part: passing away.[6]

But then we also have to ask: What other dark corners of our lives are we supposed to affirm?

14 | HISTORY

Weighing only seventy pounds, a mother collapses, worked to death in a concentration camp. A father swings lifeless from a tree, racist murderers thieving his family's land. An adolescent girl is forced to marry an elderly man, never to read a book or take a walk in solitude. Ripped away from his parents, a toddler is scarred with permanent psychological damage.

We distance ourselves from these sufferings, but we are their products. Had World War II not happened, it is likely that my mother would not have been born. (Without the war, her parents would likely not have met, married, and reproduced when they did, if at all.) Of course, that would mean that I would not have existed either. But then to be grateful for her life and mine, do I have to also be grateful for World War II? And that, of course, is just the tip of a terrible iceberg. Nearly everyone living today would not have been created were it not for the global slave trade, the theft of indigenous peoples' lands, colonialism, and the domination and extermination of whole populations, along with countless other wars, miseries, and subjugations. Had even one part of that history changed for the better, different people would have met one another, different pairs would have reproduced, and offspring different from you and me would have been created.

So except for those whose entire family tree was isolated somewhere so remote that they were all unaffected by human history's most appalling wrongs, our very lives are the highest stones on humanity's cairn of oppression. We would not have existed were it not for those brutalities, nor would our children. But then how can we who have caromed off of these sufferings and injustices affirm our lives? If I am grateful for the lives of my daughter and my mother and myself, do I have to be grateful for the Holocaust, too, given that without the Holocaust we would not have existed? Or do we have to wish that a better world had preempted ours and in the process wish away our own creation and that of our children?

Pessimists conclude that since we are inseparable from our causal origins, it all comes as a "package deal," as Saul Smilansky puts it: we either get that terrible history and us, or we get a better world that would have to preempt our existence. And since those terrible origins cannot be embraced, our own existence is problematic as well.[1] While I appreciate that line of thinking, and while I would not want to ignore history, I subscribe to a different school of thought: I am a separator, not a packager. We can affirm our lives, in the ways that we want, without affirming the grisly past that got us here. The Dalai Lama can be grateful for becoming a better person without also affirming the exile that set him on the path to self-improvement. His particular case might seem to demand packaging, because again, there is no way to fully work on being more patient without having your patience tried. But it makes sense to be glad that you've become a better person without also being glad that what forced you to become a better person was being victimized in some way. These things can pull apart axiologically if not etiologically.

So does that answer our question? Maybe affirmation can be selective in this way: we can be grateful for our lives without affirming the injustices, abuses, and other regrettable histories that were required for us to exist.

We can't accept that answer without confronting a more compelling perspective on the packager's position. Consider Derek Parfit's much-discussed case.[2] A girl decides to have a child. Being so young herself, she cannot take very good care of the child, but she does her best, and they end up with a loving mother-child bond. Many years later, the mother wonders if it was the wrong choice to have a child at fourteen years old. Her own life prospects were curtailed, and her parenting was much worse than it would have been had she waited before getting pregnant. It seems to be *obviously* the wrong choice when posed as a forward-looking question. If at the time she had asked her friends and family, "I'm thinking about getting pregnant here at fourteen years old, what do you think? Should I do it?" everyone she trusted would have said, "Wait. Having a child now would be a mistake." And yet looking back decades later, she knows that if she had waited she would not have had *that* child. She would have had a different child. The actual child that she now wholeheartedly loves never would have existed.

That love is what motivates packaging: *Wouldn't you do it all over again, in conditions more or less like the real ones that actually took place, if you were faced with such a choice?* Could a loving mother really prefer a hypothetical world where she waited and ultimately had a different child, if it would mean that she never got to spend her life with the child she now loves? Would you wipe away Hitler and Pol Pot and history's other monsters, but in so doing also wipe away your parents meeting and therefore your own conception and your own child's existence?

In my prouder moments I like to believe that I would give up my life to save history's billions from suffering. But it is easy to say that about oneself. It is much harder to say that from the mother's perspective. If she had a chance to do it all over again, wouldn't—and shouldn't—she choose to re-create her same daughter, to repeat the choice? Don't we rightly say that we wouldn't trade our children for the world? This is the hard reality behind the packaging impulse: our most meaningful attachments seem to demand an affirmation so decisive that we would create them all over again, if we faced the choice, with all that entails. The part of us where love lives insists that we keep our kids, damn the consequences.

Still, I think we should embrace selective regret and affirmation.[3] One part of this task is to identify different kinds of evaluation. Perhaps we want to say that the child's existence is good from her mother's current perspective without being good from a more neutral perspective.[4] Or perhaps there is an *impersonal* way of looking at things, where it makes sense to regret the way things have gone, but also a *personal* way of seeing things where we are glad that we and our children exist. The personal perspective looks at how actual people are actually affected, which means, importantly, that it is not a selfish perspective. As Guy Kahane points out, a better history wouldn't actually be better for the people whose suffering we wish we could undo, for *they too* would never get to exist in a better world.[5] The best history would have *wholly* different people, or likelier yet, an entire species kinder than us. We don't really want this, do we? The perspective that counsels us to care about the actual people who suffered from history's gargantuan abuses also makes it hard to comprehensively regret our past. We can't wish away the bad yesterdays without wishing away the people who we care about when we are wishing their time had been better. Luther Ingram was onto something: if loving you is wrong, I don't want to be right.

So we can say that history might be regrettable in one sense and affirmable in another. With some sort of distinction like this in hand, the second separator step is to take a stand on how our selection of partial regrets and partial affirmations fits together into one overall assessment: *Would you replay that same history all over again, if you could?*

We have two more choices. The first is to side with one half of the separation. If you're a pessimist, you might simply go with what is impersonally better and, all things considered, regret our existence in some sense. If instead you prefer a more positive take, then following Kahane you might say that morality requires us to care about actual people, which means that some version of the personal perspective should have priority over an impersonal way of looking at things. A different route to the same conclusion is to say that affirming actual history may be *rationally* if not *morally* justified.[6] Or you might determine that it makes sense to *prefer* things the way they actually are while accepting that they could have been *better* and that prior to our attachments forming it would not have made sense to prefer the sub-optimal outcome that ended up becoming our reality.[7] In any event, all of these first-option approaches conclude that all things considered, either we should or should not wish to repeat history, if that were up to us.

At the end of the day I am unable to shake my resistance to any all-things-considered assessment. This is the second approach. I am powerfully attached to my own existence, as well as my daughter's and that of the other people I love; but I am powerfully repelled by the great crimes of the past, even when I remind myself that they were necessary for our existence today. So instead of coming to some sort of resolved, wholehearted, all-things-considered final judgment about what we should prefer if we had the choice to do it all over again, I settle for the conclusion that there is no answer to the question of whether the present and its past are something that on balance we should want to re-create, if we had that power.[8] What is rational to want to do if we had the choice to do it all over again is undetermined. There is no stance from which an overall assessment can be rendered. It's not that I don't know the answer. It's that there *is* no answer.

To say this is to be torn, not neutral. While actual history is better for us in some sense, there is another sense in which it is also outrageous, and in that latter sense we ought not choose to do it all over again—all while love insistently reminds us to be thankful that we cannot make such a choice, since our lived position cements us to attachments that were born in the very trouble we wish we could undo. Neither affirmation nor regret fits this package of views. The force of commitment and care that fits an indeterminacy judgment like this leaves us in a state of active conflict.

Earlier we wondered if all-in regret jeopardizes the mother's love: Could loving parents actually wish for a better world in which their child never existed? The same sort of question applies to being torn, too. But ultimately I think that a state of conflict, as opposed to a resolved state of regret, can capture the deeply loving way that we affirm our own lives and our children's lives. More than that, it is also the kind of love we *want*. What else but love could even begin to contest the moral force of (hypothetically) saving millions from suffering or (hypothetically) securing profound personal benefits that awaited in life paths other than the one you actually chose?

Now perhaps love's power walks us right up to the place where we are tempted to decisively affirm those grotesque histories that gave us what we love, to choose it all over again regardless of the cost. I find myself unable to push across that threshold. An attachment that is fanatical, where no part of you recognizes any claims that countless others or even another version of yourself might make on your attachments, is a jealous kind of love. It is also an unnecessary love. It is enough for us to know that while our parents would always want us in their lives if given the chance to go back and do it all over again, there is also a sense in which we all might wish that history could have gone a different way.

It is not ridiculous to describe this as a wish for the impossible: to have ourselves and each other without the past that is required for ourselves and each other. But why should we demand more than that? Where is it written that full reconciliation is required when the many objects of a broad and generous love are not mutually compatible? For although it is *impossible* in a way that implicates the laws of nature and metaphysics, the wish is not *inconceivable*. We can imagine our grandparents existing and meeting in a vastly different, better world. That fantasy is enough for love to attach to. To be torn is to accept that, when reality is compromised, we would have most preferred a conceivable impossibility. Perhaps we need some sort of evaluative dialetheism, some room for moral contradiction. In the human condition, limiting our ideals to the merely possible is a luxury that conscience cannot afford.

If you disagree with this, though, I hope that you will accept two separate arguments for affirming our lives without wholly affirming the regrettable origins of our lives. First, the central claim I am making in arguing that we ought to be holistically grateful for life is that our lives are good *for us*, not that they are good for others or that they are morally justified or that they are what an impartial and benevolent observer would have chosen for a species capable of suffering pain and violation and indignity. And so, whether or not we would wish for history to be replayed so that we and our children may live, we can still be wholeheartedly, unconditionally *grateful* for our lives. This gratitude remains even when wholehearted, unconditional re-affirmation of our existence is destabilized. After all, different kinds of affirming attitudes are at our disposal.[9] More than that, we owe it to the people whose suffering made our well-being possible to find gratitude for the value in our lives.[10] If it is worth lamenting the loss of something valuable, we had better appreciate the value that the loss produced. Regret makes gratitude necessary. Anything less is an insult to those whose sacrifice made our existences possible.

Second, holistic gratitude is warranted by radiant value, where the role that an object or relationship or project plays in one of our rightly valued stories sends its positive value to the parts of that meaningful object or relationship or project. But of course the *cause* of the meaningful object or relationship or project is not a *part* of the meaningful object or relationship or project. The cause of what we value must be separate from what we value, insofar as causes and their effects are separate entities. So gratitude for the terrible conditions that led to our lives could never be justified by holistic affirmation of our lives. Parts connect to their wholes in a way that is different than the connection between causes and effects, and the part/whole connection is what is integral to holistic gratitude.

Because the past that precedes us is not connected to us as part to whole, holistic gratitude for our lives will not reach back into what made us. The affirmation of life pursued here does not compel us to affirm history's most awful wrongs. But this takes the question from outside our lives and pushes it back inside: What exactly are the parts of our lives that we are supposed to holistically affirm?

15 | EXPERIENCE

If we are going to affirm our lives, it might seem like we therefore need to affirm every experience we have. "Let us be grateful and bear in mind what has been done to us," the Buddha, Siddhartha Gautama, once said, "and let us not forget even a particle of what has been done to us." If we were to live by the literal meaning of these words, we would be grateful for every aspect of our experience—anything from a random toothache to being bullied in grade school.[1] Does holistic gratitude for life require that? Are we supposed to be grateful for every single one of our experiences, even the bad and pointless ones, on the grounds that everything that we experience is a part of our meaningful lives?

It is possible that every experience has some positive value by virtue of its connection to our lives, but I find it counter-intuitive to think that a toothache has any goodness in it, in normal circumstances at least. (Set aside special cases where dental pain reminds you to floss or teaches you how to deal with adversity.) And there is an explanation for this intuition in the story we are telling. As we saw earlier, although *parts* of meaningful goods get radiant positive value, the *contents* of those goods do not. The grateful teen-ager affirms the car's 8-track, not the skunk. Similarly, any particular experience we have is one of the contents of our existence; it is not a part of our existence in the sense that matters here. Because your valuable life stories require your existence as an experiencer, your existence as a sensitive, con-scious creature is meaningful (if you are fortunate to enjoy a life worth living). Life therefore radiates values to its parts. That does not mean that anything meaningful to you also depends either on your total set of lifetime experiences or on any particular experience considered individually. Our lives, the subjective platforms for our particular experiences, are distinct from the experiences themselves.

What is part of existing as an experiencer? The exact an-swer is just whatever it takes to be an entity that can have the relevant experiences. This includes bare biological life, the kind that a coral has, but it also includes consciousness, perception, and sensitivity, as well as the capacities for com-plex emotions, and for doing certain things, and for making choices in some sort of autonomous way. As a result, there may be several bad parts of life that get positive radiant value from life. Though that one toothache you had last week does not borrow goodness from existence, a general sensi-tivity to pain might get some of life's radiant value: if sen-sitivity to pain is a part of the sentient existence that plays a role in our valuable stories, then this sensitivity would be a part of our meaningful existence. Perhaps susceptibility to anxiety or confusion or memory are also compromised parts of life that get some radiant value from our valuable kind of existence.

Let's assume for the sake of argument that these capacities, with all of their downsides, are parts of experiential existence and so draw some of life's radiant value. Still, any particular experiences, be they good or bad, are not components of what it is to be an experiencer. And because what has radiant value is being an experiencer rather than a total set of experiences, our particular experiences do not get any of life's radiant value.

Instead, whether any specific experience will get any radiant value will depend on whether and how it *independently* connects to our valuable narratives. Is it part of a random and trivial moment in your life? Does it merely cause a later good? Or is it foundational to a treasured relationship? Is it expressive of a core part of your identity? Obviously these things have to be answered on a case-by-case basis. What we can say in general is that the meaningfulness of our existence does not itself radiate goodness out to all of our particular experiences. It spreads to the parts of our existence as experiencers, not to life's contents.

The last question, then, is whether passing away is one of those parts of our existence. If it is, then it will get some of life's radiant value and potentially be something that we can holistically affirm.

16 | THE LAST PART

If what I have said so far is correct, our lives are radiant goods, gifts for which we should feel grateful. And life's goodness spreads to the parts of our existence as experiencers—although not to the history that preceded our existence, and not to each one of our particular experiences. The final step on our third path is to determine whether one of the parts of life that gets some of its radiant value is the very end of that subjectivity: life's passing away into nonexistence.

A variation on the timing puzzle looms here. Ludwig Wittgenstein writes that "death is not an event in life: we do not live to experience death."[1] As we saw on our first path, it is certain that we do not experience death, if by "death" we mean *being* dead, that is, being in a state of non-existence that comes after subjective experience ceases. But what about passing away? Do we experience slipping into non-existence? That's a hard question to answer, given our lack of credible reports from the other side. But we do not need to answer it, since we are not trying to find goodness in any particular *experience*. Instead we simply want to know if passing away is a part of our existence. To the extent that Wittgenstein really means to talk about the "event" of becoming dead rather than the state of being dead, he seems to be suggesting that passing away is located entirely outside of life. But that is impossible, as we can see by working through the possible temporal locations of death, ruling out the unworkable ones and isolating the viable ones.

One option to consider is that passing away happens once we no longer exist. But as we also saw on the first path, passing away can't be wholly contained in our non-existence, for then it would have to precede itself—the event in which we become dead not happening until we have already become dead. That is impossible.

Another option is that passing away happens in some episode between existence and non-existence. In that scenario again, passing away would not be a part of our existence, and the argument we are pursuing would not work. But this way of seeing things requires that we can be in a state other than existence or non-existence. Like passing away after one has already passed away, I think it is reasonable to say that this is impossible, too.

So since passing away cannot be wholly contained in our non-existence, and since it is not in some impossible gap between existence and nonexistence, it seems that passing away has to be found, at least in part, in our lives. (Note that passing away can't be, say, the combination of the last moment of existence and the first moment of non-existence, for then again part of passing away would have to happen after one has already passed away—after one already has become nonexistent—which is impossible.) That leaves two possible relationships between life and passing away. First, passing away might be the very last event that happens during our existence. This pretty clearly makes it a part of life. Or, second, passing away might lie right on the line between the last moment of existence and the first moment of non-existence.

In this second analysis, passing away is not found *during* life's last moment. Instead it would be the joint that connects two immediately adjacent moments. Strictly speaking, then, we would pass away neither inside the time during which we live, nor outside of it either. Passing away would be located right on the precipice of non-existence. Like a seam that joins two immediately adjacent objects in space, or a border between two states that doesn't take up any of its very own land, passing away would not occupy any temporal location of its own. The location of the seam *just is* where the two objects join. Consequently, this way of understanding passing away has it being part of *both* existence and non-existence, rather than in between them (which, again, is impossible).

It's hard to know what to think of this view. It is confusing to think that something might simultaneously be part of two things that are entirely separate from each other. So you (like me) might find yourself pushing back against this idea. But if you resist it, remember that the only option left is that passing away happens to us during our last moment of existence. These are the only two theories that even approach coherence. They are the only two possibilities meeting that minimum threshold to be contenders.

I'm not sure which of the two is correct, but for our purposes it doesn't really matter. These two viable interpretations of passing away both have passing away being a part of mortal existence. It is located either *during* the last moment of existence, or *at* the outermost edge of that moment. Either way, passing away is a part of our existence (and part of non-existence, too, if the seam theory is correct). It can't be anywhere else. As commonsense would insist, passing away appears to be the *last* thing that happens to us, not something that happens *after* we die.

Passing away will deprive us of too much to measure. But the void that death leaves in the world also frames our lives' presence. That framing means that if life is a radiant good, then passing away has some goodness, too, drawn from the very life that it drains. The boundary of our subjectivity, like the edge of the stage on which a play is performed, is as much a part of the show as anything else, and for that it basks in its value.

And just as the 8-track and the ugliness in Grandma's sweater do not contribute any value to the radiantly good whole, so the parts of life, including passing away, need not contribute anything to life's positive value. These things *acquire* positive value by being parts of meaningful pieces in your life's stories, but they don't have to *add* value of their own. Passing away can be a useless appendage. Worse, it looks like it is a bad deprivation. Still, as long as it is part of the radiant good of life, passing away takes value from the whole. It need not give value, too.

That said, as a separate issue maybe death can sometimes *also* contribute its own additional value. Certain deaths do appear to play essential roles in valuable narratives. Consider the musician Col. Bruce Hampton, who died on stage during the closing moments of a concert honoring his seventieth birthday as he and an all-star tribute band were hitting the peak of their finale, "Turn on Your Love Light." To a distanced observer like me, that sounds like a pretty good way to go out for someone with his kind of life. His life story arguably had some extra value because of the *manner* of his death—the way in which he died was, arguably at least, a "good death" for a musician like him, just as a warrior might think that a good death would be dying valiantly in battle.

Dale Dorsey says that having a good death like this makes death good.[2] I am advocating for something different. Having a poetic ending, an ending that figures in one of our valued stories, arguably makes the *way* in which we die better; it doesn't make passing away *itself* better. Dorsey points out that if someone in Hampton's position had had a more routine death, it would not be as meaningful to his story as it is for him to die in the way that he did. This sounds right. But still, that does not decide whether his story is made more meaningful by his special way of going out or instead by the mere fact that his life was extinguished. On my view, his story as someone called to a life in music was better for having his kind of death, better than it would have been had he died from a fall in the shower that same day. But it does not make the fact that he died any better.

Another way that one's manner of death might contribute its own value to one's life is that, without our deaths, our lives would be *different lives*.[3] A story with a different ending is a different story, and this can impact value. My grandfather's life might have been better in one respect had he lived long enough to meet his great-granddaughter; but the actual life he had, where he did not get to meet her, was valuable, too, and his actual life would not have been *that* life, with *that* meaning and *that* value, had he lived long enough to meet his great-granddaughter. So to whatever extent we value our actual stories, perhaps we should value the goodness in them as defined by the way they actually go. And since passing away helps determine how our lives go, it might contribute some extra value of its own by playing this defining role in our stories.

But at the same time, it is also possible that a life with a different death could have a value comparable to the value that person gets from their actual life with their actual death. It is therefore important that we center our focus on the main point: even if death doesn't contribute any value of its own, it still is a part of life. And since life is a meaningful good, at least for those with lives worth living, that is enough for passing away to draw some positive value of its own from our lives.

What makes passing away an affliction is that it is the part of our fates that in one shot rips away all of our valuable opportunities. But in depriving us this way, passing away makes itself a part—the last part—of the lives that it ends. That laces it with radiant value from the meaningful good that is our kind of existence.

17 | SOLACE

Like many others who are diagnosed with a life-threatening illness, my mom saw her cancer as an opportunity to appreciate life anew, to focus on being grateful for everything good that she had. Once this project was underway, she excelled at finding her gratitude even when things got ugly.

From that perspective, a special set of values comes into relief. From the standpoint of gratitude, we don't evaluate what we have by comparing it to some better thing that we didn't get. Gratitude means comparing the gifts we get to their most radical, most existential alternative: never getting the gift to begin with. That is one reason why the teenager would seem ungrateful if she complained about the car's stereo. *Just be thankful you have a car at all.*

When we adopt the standpoint of being grateful for life, we compare it not to a better life or an immortal life but instead to the very real possibility that at any moment we could have been robbed of its ongoing goodness. The existential alternative that gratitude brings into focus is that we could have lived lives that were much shorter or had much less value than the lives we actually got to live. The existential alternative for life's gifts is not having enjoyed them. At the limit, those who think that being created is a benefit will want to insist that the ultimate existential alternative is never having been created in the first place.

We didn't have to end up here, at this moment we are in right now. Far from it. The number of unlikely convergences required for us to have been created and then to have subsequently enjoyed our lives is famously preposterous. The earth settles just a bit farther from the sun, and there is no us. Or any one of your ancestors trips over a wrinkle in the fabric of history and finds themselves attracted to a different person, or gets pregnant a few months later, or gets swept up in any number of other possibilities, and there is no you. Someone else takes your place. And then, once we have been created, it only multiplies the unlikelihoods for us to get to live out our lives in the manner we do. You walk down a different street, a politician starts the wrong war, or your nurse washes his hands in a slightly different way, and death calls your number much earlier than it otherwise would have. From the perspective of gratitude for life, to die is to have lived, and to have lived a valuable life is to be incalculably lucky. That value gets renewed every moment.[1]

Everything I have said so far, then, seems to point toward one conclusion: we should be grateful for passing away. After all, I am claiming that life is a meaningful good, so life's bad parts, including passing away, get radiant goodness. And since the appropriate attitude to have toward a valuable and meaningful life is holistic gratitude, then is the conclusion that we should be grateful for our mortality because it has some of life's radiant goodness?

I actually think that is not quite right. While we can be holistically grateful for bad things, remember that if a part of something meaningful is overwhelmingly bad overall, then holistic gratitude can be rendered unfitting. Even if they love their adult son, and even if he plays a meaningful role in their own lives, Hitler's parents should not be grateful for his awful qualities. And you might not be grateful for your lover's lack of patience. Tremendous negative value can swamp radiant positive value and consequently impact which attitudes are most appropriate. In particular, because *gratitude* is so enthusiastic and univocal, it has a limited range of application. (Begrudging gratitude—*Thanks, er, I guess*—seems to be a disjointed attitude.) When a towering mountain of bad sits next to a mere heap of goodness, what is needed is an affirmation less full throated than gratitude.

The deprivations of death dominate the radiant goodness that passing away draws from life, making gratitude a poor fit for our mortality. But that doesn't mean that we have to avoid *all* kinds of affirmation. On the contrary, even in the face of its terrible deprivations, the radiant value that passing away draws from life seems to deserve some sort of recognition. We need an affirmation that respects death's grave injury but also acknowledges its position as part of one of our most cherished goods, the good of life. What is called for is something between the extremes of unalloyed gratitude and unadulterated dread.

I believe that this more fitting affirmation is just what we have been searching for: solace. Solace is the attitude we can take toward death when, amid all the reasons it gives us to be afraid and despondent, we attend to the radiant value that it gathers from life. When there is so much badness, we don't expect to find bliss. We don't demand unbridled joy or hope for wholehearted cheer. We just want to find some comfort.

Return one last time to the teenager. Imagine now that even though she doesn't complain, you can tell that she is a little disappointed about not having the kind of car stereo she wants. She doesn't feel entitled to it, and she would never say anything about it; but being able to read her well, you know that she wishes she had it all the same. If you were to approach her with compassion in this moment, how might you offer a little comfort? One thing you might try to do is to focus on the positive, to help her find gratitude in the fact that she is fortunate to have a car, to attend to what she has rather than what she lacks. This kind of consolation does not come from replenishing her hope that the better thing will come one day, if she just works hard enough or waits long enough or wins the lottery. It comes from realizing that she already has it pretty good, and that the banged-up parts of her car are worth cherishing in their own broken way.

This is the kind of comfort we can find in the relationship between life and passing away. It doesn't matter what your valuable life looked like or how it will end. The religious and the nonreligious, the young and the old, people from every walk of life, all can have deaths with this value. As long as you have had a life worth living, you will get a piece of radiant goodness at the end of that life.

If this is right, then while passing away is bad, it does not have to loom so menacingly over us. The distress we feel when we focus on what death costs us can rationally give way to an equanimity embedded in being grateful for life, the kind of relaxed contentment that comes with greeting something that has been sitting next to us every day as an inextricable price of the things we value most. The final thread in our outermost seam waits, visible. That edge, the line that gives our particular lives their shape, can be recognized, validated, acknowledged, even embraced. It might help give some meaning to our lives. Or it might not. Either way, it is enough that part of the tapestry is its boundary, for each part of the tapestry gets a share of the whole's value even when those parts considered in isolation lack any beauty of their own.

This was what I wanted to talk about with my mom. It is rational to fear death. Its bad aspects can be overwhelming. When our limit eventually propels us into a sea of perfect deprivation, we lose the self whose subjectivity is the stage for all other goods. In being extinguished we are permanently sealed off from any field of valuable opportunity. But still, because passing away is a part of life, I wanted to tell her, there is also a comfort to be found amid the hardships of passing away. By reminding ourselves of how fortunate we are to live the lives that passing away ends, we implicate passing away in those lives, and that can help validate one of our most confusing aspirations: while we know that passing away is terrible, it might also be something in which we can reasonably find some peace. We can take solace.

18 | THE CONVERSATION

And so this is where I want to tell you about how when I next visited my mom, we finally had a meaningful conversation about death. I want to replay for you how we chatted into the night about gratitude and value and loss, about life sharing its goodness with passing away. I want to report how she took some comfort from it all.

But I had made the oldest mistake you can make when someone you love is dying: I had waited. I did not want to press a topic that scared her. I didn't want to say something foolish or worse, insensitive to what may have become her deepest vulnerability. Unable to figure out how to reassure her on both an emotional and a cognitive level at the same time, I tended to sadness and fear with avoidance. An irrational and vain desire also played a part: I wondered if maybe I could rush these thoughts that you have been reading into print before she died. The way I saw it, Mom might not want to talk about death, but she would get a kick out of reading this.

Things never got that far. Soon after the heart surgery gave her that boost, her deterioration resumed its inexorable schedule. I was urged to cancel my trip to the Tucson conference and instead fly back to Portland. And so I found myself winding one more time through its dark and wooded winter roads to the hospital that had become our house of hope and fear.

They had moved her into hospice care, and by the time I got to her room she had lost the power to speak. Nods and grunts, effortful grins and grimaces, faint hand gestures—these were the only tools of communication she had left. With conversation between us now closed off, my sins of delay sat with me in the sticky vinyl chair next to her bed, thundering amid the periodic beeps and hydraulic whooshes that have become our soundtrack to dying. Unable to talk to me about death or anything else, framed by tubes and machines and the soulless surroundings of temporary quarters, my mom just lay there, enveloped in silence.

But although she could not talk, they said she could still hear, and we were encouraged to speak to her. It was only then, too late, that I tried to offer her that little portion of solace, to give voice to the possibility that even passing away can borrow traces of goodness from the life that she and I have each been lucky enough to enjoy.

The years since that January have coated my memory in a watery blur, but what I recall happening next is that as she tilted her head back, her hand grazed mine, and, with eyes shut, she curled a fragile half-smile.

ACKNOWLEDGMENTS

This book is drawn from a pair of lectures, titled "Gratitude, Life, and Death," that were supported by the American Philosophical Association's Baumgardt Memorial Fellowship. As the Baumgardt Lectures are expressly designed to be public, this gave me a rare chance to try to present new ideas in the philosophies of death and gratitude and value in a way that might simultaneously engage a wider general audience. For that opportunity and support, I am grateful to the APA, as well as Thaine Stearns and Manuel Vargas. For vigorous discussion at those lectures, I am grateful to the two audiences at Sonoma State University. And much appreciation goes to Lucy Randall at Oxford University Press for seeing that the lectures could become a book, and to Lucy, Hannah Doyle, and the rest of the team at OUP for shepherding it to its present form.

For taking the time to give me helpful critical and expansionary comments on distant and recent ancestors of this book, I am grateful to Ben Bradley, Steve Luper, Michael Lynch, Sean McAleer, Ann Murphy, Doug Portmore, Saul Smilansky, Mark Timmons, and Aaron Wolf, as well as the students in the Lab for Advanced Ethics Research at Sonoma State University during the 2017–18 academic year, Kayla Brown, David Burkhalter, Elizabeth Cardenas, and Vanessa McMillon-Vanbuskirk. Two reviewers for OUP, one of whom I learned to be John Martin Fischer and one who remains anonymous to me, also provided valuable feedback on the manuscript. Thanks also go to Jay Wallace for conversation that helped shape my thinking on the issues taken up in Chapter 14. For helping me remember crucial details and piece together some history, I'm grateful to my brother, Andrew Glasgow; my uncle, Jack Vonfeld; and my aunt, Michèle Vonfeld. And for helpful feedback, conversations, and support along the way, special thanks go to Julie Shulman.

Finally and obviously, this book would be impossible without my mom, Renée Vonfeld Glasgow. For her support of the project, for her model of grace under pressure, and of course for her love, gratitude is not enough.

NOTES

CHAPTER 2

1. Epicurus (1940, 31).
2. Nagel (1979). See also Bradley (2009); Brueckner & Fischer (1986); Draper (1999); Feinberg (1993); Feldman (1994); Fischer (2009); McMahan (1993).
3. For more on the problem of the subject, see, e.g., Belshaw (2009); Bradley (2009); Feinberg (1993); Fischer (2009); Nagel (1979); Nussbaum (1994, ch. 6); Olson (2013, 67); Rosenbaum (1993a; 1993b); Ruben (1988); Silverstein (1993); Yourgrau (1993).

CHAPTER 3

1. Olson (2013).
2. I'm simplifying and writing as if what's bad for us is what's harmful, and what's harmful is what's bad for us. These are not identical, strictly speaking.
3. For more on this view, see Lamont (1998); Luper (2009, 70–1); Luper (2016); Wolf (2018). I'm not examining whether we might *also* be harmed by death's deprivations after we have passed away or in a timeless manner. For recent explorations of these views, see Bradley (2009); Feit (2002); Feldman (1994, ch. 9); McMahan (1993; 2002, ch. 2); Purves (2017).
4. Johansson (2014, 150). For more discussion of the standard objection to concurrentism, also see Bradley (2009, 89); Broome (2013, 220); Feldman (1994, 153–4); Grey (1999); Johansson (2013, 261); Li (1999); Purves (2017, 812).
5. Sen (1993).
6. Feldman (1994, 137).

7. Cf. Rosati (2013a).

CHAPTER 4

1. Lucretius (1987, 81). For analysis of what exactly Lucretius was doing, see Warren (2004, ch. 3).
2. Fischer (2009); Finocchiaro & Sullivan (2016, 155).
3. Deng (2015, 420); Luper (2009, 63); Luper (2016, sec. 3.2).
4. This explanation for our asymmetrical attitudes toward creation and extinction is compatible with several of the other answers out there, such as that future goods matter more to us than do past goods (Brueckner & Fischer 1986) or that modifying one's creation date compromises personal identity, personal history, or personal character in a way that modifying one's date of death does not (Belshaw 1993; Kaufman 1996; Nagel 1979).

CHAPTER 5

1. Scheffler (2013, 101). See also Bradley (2009, sec. 2.3).

CHAPTER 6

1. E.g., Bradley (2009, 63); McMahan (2002, 103–4); Purves (2017, 799–819). Thanks to Kayla Brown for helpful discussion here.
2. Nagel (1986, 224). For the argument that infinitely wanting one's life extended is not identical to wanting one's life infinitely extended, see Moore (2006) and Coren (2018). Coren provides a nice analogy: every day you can want to eat whatever you want without worrying about the health consequences, but that is not the same as wanting it to be true that every day you eat whatever you want without worrying about the health consequences. Warren (2004, 71–3) holds that we are not deprived by not living for millennia, because it is not reasonable to hope to live that long. But we can be deprived by death as long as we experience attachment (Draper 1999), and attachment can go forever.

3. Cf. Benatar (2017, 107, 134). Thanks to Ben Bradley for helpful conversation here.
4. Kamm (1993, 16). For a dramatic depiction of this phenomenon, see David Blumenfeld's (2009, 384–5) story of "John."

CHAPTER 7
1. Borges (1964, 114). See also Williams (1973); Kagan (2012, ch. 11); May (2009, ch. 2).
2. Fischer (2009, 83–90); Fischer & Mitchell-Yellin (2014); cf. Benatar (2017, ch. 6); Chappell (2007).
3. Belshaw (2015); Bortolotti (2010); Greene (2017); Moore (2006, 318 n. 14); Nozick (1981, 579n); Temkin (2008, 204).
4. Chappell (2007, 39); Fischer (2009, 89–90); Kolodny (2013, 166); McMahan (2002, 101); Scarre (2007, 56–7); Temkin (2008).
5. Beglin (2017); Cave (2012, 266); Jones (2015); Lenman (1995); May (2009, ch. 2); Nussbaum (1994, ch. 6); Scheffler (2013, ch. 3); and drawing from Heidegger, Sigrist (2015). Nussbaum (1999; 2013) has since moderated her view.
6. Ismael (2006).
7. Nussbaum (1994, 227–9).
8. Burley (2009, 537–8); Lenman (1995); May (2009, 88); Nussbaum (2013, 42); Temkin (2008, 206–7).
9. Beglin (2017, 2019–20).
10. Ferrero (2015); Fischer (2009, 122, 160); Fischer (2013, 345–6); Kolodny (2013, 167); Nussbaum (1999, 812).
11. Bortolotti (2010); Chappell (2007); Fischer & Mitchell-Yellin (2014, 367–8); Kolodny (2013, 167); Nozick (1981, 580); cf. Raz (2001, 86).
12. Ismael (2006). For a variation on Ismael's argument, see Malpas (1998). For a variation on our response, see Ferrero (2015).
13. Glasgow (2013).

CHAPTER 8
1. Beardsley (1965); Kagan (1998); Kahane (2014); O'Neill (1992).

2. Nussbaum (2013, 37).
3. Paul (2014); cf. Sullivan (2018, 162).

CHAPTER 9

1. Emmons (2007); Watkins (2004); Emmons & McCullough (2003); see also Wood et al. (2010); Rind and Bordia (1995); Clark et al. (1988).
2. Fitzgerald (1998); Boleyn-Fitzgerald (2016).
3. There are other interesting cases where what we are grateful for does not benefit us. Smilansky (1997) thinks that we should be grateful to people for merely not harming us: to avoid spoiling our environment with your trash takes your effort and concern for others, just as benefitting people does. And Walker (1980–81) presents us with the case of being grateful to your daughter's teacher for taking an interest in her development. I take it that in this sort of case we bear the emotional, reactive responsibility for our children's benefits. It seems that attitudes can be delegated to others on our behalf.
4. Fitzgerald (1998, 126).

CHAPTER 10

1. I am grateful to Steven Luper for suggesting the skunk comparison. A real estate agent once told me that what comes with a purchased house—what is part of the house, as opposed to the contents that the previous owners can take with them—is anything that would stay attached if you picked up the house and turned it upside down. That principle is probably more helpful for transactions than for metaphysics: I'm pretty sure that if you staple the skunk carcass to the car, it's still not a part of the car.
2. Similarly, some objects gain their social (as opposed to personal) significance because of their role in valuable histories, such as the pen Lincoln used to sign the Emancipation Proclamation (Kagan 1998).

3. There are multiple ways of understanding narrative value. Here I follow Dorsey (2017); see also Rosati (2013b). The distinctive value of meaningful goods is closely allied with sentimental value, but the two are different. Whereas an object has sentimental value for us only if we have the right emotional stance or sentiments about it (Hatzimoysis 2003), this is not required for a good to be meaningful in the sense operative for us here. As for the other direction, does anything with sentimental value have to be meaningful in our sense? Possibly, but I suspect not: a sentimental attachment to a memento that has no connection to other parts of one's life might be odd, but that does not make it impossible.

CHAPTER 11
1. *Good Will Hunting* (1997).

CHAPTER 12
1. Moore (1903, esp. sec. 18–22). Thanks to Sean McAleer and Mark Timmons for helpful discussion related to what follows.
2. Hurka (2014, 65–9). Also see Hurka (1998), where he finds that when our attitudes—in particular, care and admiration—are directed at the part, the analysis we are pursuing fits better than Moore's (though the Moorean analysis may well fit other cases [cf. Bradley 2002]). If what I suggest is on track, affirmations in general, and gratitude in particular, are a branch of attitudes that follow this pattern.

CHAPTER 13
1. Here I'm blurring the distinction between being better off never having existed and having a life not worth living. For a more subtle treatment of these distinct ideas, see Smilansky (2007, ch. 10). As noted in Chapter 6, there is a case to be made that even this baby is harmed by death, if eventually science would cure the baby of her misery and enable her to live for a blissful eternity.

2. Nagel (1979, 2).
3. Baillie (2019).
4. Henry Sidgwick (1890, 248 n. 1) argued that life is only valuable if it is a *happy* life, in which case life is not *unconditionally* good. This offers a reminder of the limits of our argument. Life's radiant value does not mean that life is unconditionally good; the argument only applies to those with lives worth living. Nor is life *non-relationally* good. On the contrary, a meaningful good must be relationally valued, since narrativity is a function of relations between isolated features or episodes. So life might be a conditional and relational good and still be the most meaningful good we have. For a more sustained argument that life is neither intrinsically nor unconditionally good, see Raz (2001, ch. 3).
5. McConnell (1993, 211).
6. McMahan (1993, 236–7). For a defense of anti-natalism, see Benatar (2008). For one response to anti-natalism that dovetails with our line here that life is actually pretty good, see Smilansky (2012). Finally, see Johansson (2010) for a helpful discussion of the puzzle that existence seemingly cannot be better for us than non-existence because, first, existence being better for us implies that non-existence would be worse for us, and, second, nothing can be worse (or better) for someone who never exists.

CHAPTER 14

1. Smilansky (2013). In a similar vein, Robert Adams (2006, 246) writes that "finding positive value in actual human projects . . . involves some sort of acceptance of the causal nexus they presuppose, some acceptance of the actual causal structure of human life"; and R. Jay Wallace (2013) thinks that the kind of unconditional affirmation we want for ourselves and our loved ones demands an affirmation of the history that produced us. And since we can't unconditionally affirm history's misery, Smilansky concludes that our existence is regrettable, while Wallace finds the human condition absurd.

2. Parfit (1984, 358–9).

3. For more on the separator perspective, see Bagnoli (2016); Jones (2017); Lenman (2017, 426–7); Metz (2009); Reginster (2016); Woodward (1986).

4. Jones (2017).

5. Kahane (2019); see also Adams (1979) and Adams (2006).

6. Bagnoli (2016).

7. Harman (2009).

8. Cf. Adams (1979).

9. Kolodny (2016, 776); Wallace (2016, 805).

10. Reginster (2016, 791).

CHAPTER 15

1. The Buddha quote is from Streng (1989, 49). Streng offers an alternative interpretation, where gratitude is encouraged only toward those who have aided in one's Buddhist development.

CHAPTER 16

1. Wittgenstein (1961, 6:4311); cf. Mothershill (1987, 86); Teichman (1993, 157).

2. Dorsey (2017).

3. Fischer (2013); Ismael (2006).

CHAPTER 17

1. Something similar to this seems to be Zilai's reasoning in the *Zhuangzi* (2009, 45–6). I am grateful to Sean McAleer for pointing me to this text. See also Wallace (2013, ch. 4) for an argument that affirming one's life means contrasting it with the alternative of never having lived. And for an analysis of contentment and gratitude that suggests that it is virtuous to adopt something like the picture of gratitude being presented here, see Calhoun (2018, ch. 7).

REFERENCES

Adams, Robert Merrihew. 1979. "Existence, Self-Interest, and the Problem of Evil." *Noûs* 13, 53–65.

Adams, Robert Merrihew. 2006. "Love and the Problem of Evil." *Philosophia* 34, 243–51.

Bagnoli, Carla. 2016. "Rooted in the Past, Hooked in the Present: Vulnerability to Contingency and Immunity to Regret." *Philosophy and Phenomenological Research* 92, 763–70.

Baillie, James. 2019. "The Recognition of Nothingness." *Philosophical Studies*, online first, 1–19.

Beardsley, Monroe C. 1965. "Intrinsic Value." *Philosophy and Phenomenological Research* 26, 1–17.

Beglin, David. 2017. "Should I Choose to Never Die? Williams, Boredom, and the Meaning of Mortality." *Philosophical Studies* 174, 2009–28.

Belshaw, Christopher. 1993. "Asymmetry and Nonexistence." *Philosophical Studies* 70, 103–16.

Belshaw, Christopher. 2009. *Annihilation: The Sense and Meaning of Death*. Stocksfield: Acumen.

Belshaw, Christopher. 2015. "Immortality, Memory and Imagination." *Journal of Ethics* 19, 323–48.

Benatar, David. 2008. *Better Never to Have Been*. Oxford: Oxford University Press.

Benatar, David. 2017. *The Human Predicament*. Oxford: Oxford University Press.

Blumenfeld, David. 2009. "Living Life over Again." *Philosophy and Phenomenological Research* 79, 357–86.

Boleyn-Fitzgerald, Patrick. 2016. "Gratitude toward Things." In *Perspectives on Gratitude: An Interdisciplinary Approach*, edited by David Carr (London: Routledge), 112–25.

Borges, Jorge Luis. 1964. "The Immortal." In *Labyrinths: Selected Stories & Other Writings*, edited by Donald A. Yates & James E. Irby (New York: New Directions), 105–18.

Bortolotti, Lisa. 2010. "Agency, Life Extension, and the Meaning of Life." *The Monist* 93, 38–56.

Bradley, Ben. 2002. "Is Intrinsic Value Conditional?" *Philosophical Studies* 107, 23–44.

Bradley, Ben. 2009. *Well-Being and Death*. Oxford: Oxford University Press.

Broome, John. 2013. "The Badness of Death and the Goodness of Life." In *The Oxford Handbook of Philosophy of Death*, edited by Ben Bradley, Fred Feldman, & Jens Johansson (Oxford: Oxford University Press), 218–33.

Brueckner, Anthony L., & Fischer, John Martin. 1986. "Why Is Death Bad?" *Philosophical Studies* 50, 213–21.

Burley, Mikel. 2009. "Immortality and Meaning: Reflections on the Makropulos Debate." *Philosophy* 84, 529–47.

Calhoun, Cheshire. 2018. *Doing Valuable Time: The Present, the Future, and Meaningful Living*. Oxford: Oxford University Press.

Cave, Stephen. 2012. *Immortality*. New York: Crown Publishers.

Chappell, Timothy. 2007. "Infinity Goes upon Trial: Must Immortality Be Meaningless?" *European Journal of Philosophy* 17, 30–44.

Clark, H. B., Northrop, J. T., & Barkshire, C.T. 1988. "The Effects of Contingent Thank-You Notes on Case Managers' Visiting Residential Clients." *Education and Treatment of Children* 11, 45–51.

Coren, Daniel. 2018. "Always Choose to Live or Choose to Always Live?" *Southwest Philosophy Review* 34(2): 89–104.

Deng, Natalja. 2015. "How A-Theoretic Deprivationists Should Respond to Lucretius." *Journal of the American Philosophical Association* 1, 417–32.

Dorsey, Dale. 2017. "A Good Death." *Utilitas* 29, 153–74.

Draper, Kai. 1999. "Disappointment, Sadness, and Death." *The Philosophical Review* 108, 387–414.

Emmons, Robert A. 2007. *Thanks! How the New Science of Gratitude Can Make You Happier*. Boston: Houghton Mifflin.

Emmons, R. A., & McCullough, M. E. 2003. "Counting Blessings versus Burdens: An Experimental Investigation of Gratitude and Subjective Well-Being in Daily Life." *Journal of Personality and Social Psychology* 84(2): 377–89.

Epicurus. 1940. "Letter to Menoeceus." In *The Stoic and Epicurean Philosophers*, edited by Whitney J. Oates (New York: Modern Library), 30–3.

Feinberg, Joel. 1993. "Harm to Others." In *The Metaphysics of Death*, edited by John Martin Fischer (Stanford, CA: Stanford University Press), 171–90.

Feit, Neil. 2002. "The Time of Death's Misfortune." *Noûs* 36, 359–83.

Feldman, Fred. 1994. *Confrontations with the Reaper*. Oxford: Oxford University Press.

Ferrero, Luca. 2015. "Agency, Scarcity, and Mortality." *Journal of Ethics* 19, 349–78.

Finocchiaro, Peter, & Sullivan, Meghan. 2016. "Yet Another 'Epicurean' Argument." *Philosophical Perspectives* 30, 135–59.

Fischer, John Martin. 2009. *Our Stories: Essays on Life, Death, and Free Will*. Oxford: Oxford University Press.

Fischer, John Martin. 2013. "Immortality." In *The Oxford Handbook of Philosophy of Death*, edited by Ben Bradley, Fred Feldman, & Jens Johansson (Oxford: Oxford University Press), 336–54.

Fischer, John Martin, & Mitchell-Yellin, Benjamin. 2014. "Immortality and Boredom." *Journal of Ethics* 18, 353–72.

Fitzgerald, Patrick. 1998. "Gratitude and Justice." *Ethics* 109, 119–53.

Glasgow, Joshua. 2013. "The Shape of a Life and the Value of Loss and Gain." *Philosophical Studies* 162, 665–82.

Good Will Hunting. 1997. Directed by Gus Van Sant. Be Limited Partnership, Lawrence Bender Productions, and Miramax. Film.

Greene, Preston. 2017. "Value in Very Long Lives." *Journal of Moral Philosophy* 14, 416–34.

Grey, William. 1999. "Epicurus and the Harm of Death." *Australasian Journal of Philosophy* 77, 358–64.

Harman, Elizabeth. 2009. "'I'll Be Glad I Did It': Reasoning and the Significance of Future Desires." *Philosophical Perspectives* 23, 177–99.

Hatzimoysis, Anthony. 2003. "Sentimental Value." *The Philosophical Quarterly* 53, 373–9.

Hurka, Thomas. 1998. "Two Kinds of Organic Unity." *The Journal of Ethics* 2, 299–320.

Hurka, Thomas. 2014. *British Ethical Theorists from Sidgwick to Ewing.* Oxford: Oxford University Press.

Ismael, Jenann. 2006. "The Ethical Importance of Death." In *Death and Anti-Death,* Volume 4: *Twenty Years after De Beauvoir, Thirty Years after Heidegger,* edited by Charles Tandy (Palo Alto, CA: Ria University Press), 181–98.

Johansson, Jens. 2010. "Being and Betterness." *Utilitas* 22, 285–302.

Johansson, Jens. 2013. "The Timing Problem." In *The Oxford Handbook of Philosophy of Death,* edited by Ben Bradley, Fred Feldman, & Jens Johansson (Oxford: Oxford University Press), 255–73.

Johansson, Jens. 2014. "When Do We Incur Mortal Harm?" In *The Cambridge Companion to Life and Death,* edited by Steven Luper (Cambridge: Cambridge University Press), 149–64.

Jones, Karen. 2017. "Regret and Affirmation." *Journal of Applied Philosophy* 34, 414–9.

Jones, Ward E. 2015. "Venerating Death." *Philosophical Papers* 44, 61–81.

Kagan, Shelly. 1998. "Rethinking Intrinsic Value." *The Journal of Ethics* 2, 277–97.

Kagan, Shelly. 2012. *Death.* New Haven, CT: Yale University Press.

Kahane, Guy. 2014. "Our Cosmic Insignificance." *Noûs* 48, 745–72.

Kahane, Guy. 2019. "History and Persons." *Philosophy and Phenomenological Research* 99, 162–87.

Kamm, F. M. 1993. *Morality, Mortality, Vol. 1*. Oxford: Oxford University Press.

Kaufman, Frederik. 1996. "Death and Deprivation: Or, Why Lucretius' Symmetry Argument Fails." *Australasian Journal of Philosophy* 74, 305–12.

Kolodny, Niko. 2013. "That I Should Die and Others Live." In Samuel Scheffler, *Death & the Afterlife*, edited by Niko Kolodny (Oxford: Oxford University Press), 159–73.

Kolodny, Niko. 2016. "Dynamics of Affirmation." *Philosophy and Phenomenological Research* 92, 771–7.

Lamont, Julian. 1998. "A Solution to the Puzzle of When Death Harms Its Victims." *Australasian Journal of Philosophy* 76, 198–212.

Lenman, James. 1995. "Immortality: A Letter." *Cogito* 9, 164–9.

Lenman, James. 2017. "La Révolution Est un Bloc? Wallace on Affirmation and Regret." *Journal of Applied Philosophy* 34, 420–8.

Li, Jack. 1999. "Commentary on Lamont's When Death Harms Its Victims." *Australasian Journal of Philosophy* 77, 349–57.

Lucretius. 1987. "We Have Nothing to Fear in Death." In *Life and Meaning: A Reader*, edited by Oswald Hanfling (Oxford: Blackwell), 79–82.

Luper, Steven. 2009. *The Philosophy of Death*. Cambridge: Cambridge University Press.

Luper, Steven. 2016. "Death." *The Stanford Encyclopedia of Philosophy* (Summer 2016 Edition), Edward N. Zalta (ed.), <https://plato.stanford.edu/archives/sum2016/entries/death/>.

Malpas, Jeff. 1998. "Death and the Unity of a Life." In *Death and Philosophy*, edited by J. E. Malpas and Robert C. Solomon (London: Routledge), 120–34.

May, Todd. 2009. *Death*. Stocksfield: Acumen.

McConnell, Terrance. 1993. *Gratitude*. Philadelphia: Temple University Press.

McMahan, Jeff. 1993. "Death and the Value of Life." In *The Metaphysics of Death*, edited by John Martin Fischer (Stanford, CA: Stanford University Press), 233–66.

McMahan, Jeff. 2002. *The Ethics of Killing: Problems at the Margins of Life*. Oxford: Oxford University Press.

Metz, Thaddeus. 2009. "Love and Emotional Reactions to Necessary Evils." In *The Positive Function of Evil*, edited by Pedro Alexis Tabensky (New York: Palgrave Macmillan), 28–44.

Moore, A. W. 2006. "Williams, Nietzsche, and the Meaninglessness of Immortality." *Mind* 115, 311–30.

Moore, G. E. 1903. *Principia Ethica*. Cambridge: University Press.

Mothershill, Mary. 1987. "Death." In *Life and Meaning*, edited by Oswald Hanfling (Oxford: Blackwell), 83–92.

Nagel, Thomas. 1979. "Death." In Nagel, *Mortal Questions* (Cambridge: Cambridge University Press), 1–10.

Nagel, Thomas. 1986. *The View from Nowhere*. Oxford: Oxford University Press.

Nozick, Robert. 1981. *Philosophical Explanations*. Cambridge, MA: The Belknap Press.

Nussbaum, Martha. 1994. *The Therapy of Desire*. Princeton, NJ: Princeton University Press.

Nussbaum, Martha. 1999. "Reply to Papers in Symposium on Nussbaum, *The Therapy of Desire*," *Philosophy and Phenomenological Research* 59, 811–19.

Nussbaum, Martha. 2013. "The Damage of Death: Incomplete Arguments and False Consolations." In *The Ethics and Metaphysics of Death*, edited by James Stacey Taylor (Oxford: Oxford University Press): 25–43.

Olson, Eric T. 2013. "The Epicurean View of Death." *Journal of Ethics* 17, 65–78.

O'Neill, John. 1992. "The Varieties of Intrinsic Value." *The Monist* 75, 119–37.

Parfit, Derek. 1984. *Reasons and Persons*. Oxford: Oxford University Press.

Paul, L. A. 2014. *Transformative Experience*. Oxford: Oxford University Press.

Purves, Duncan. 2017. "Desire Satisfaction, Death, and Time." *Canadian Journal of Philosophy* 47, 799–819.

Raz, Joseph. 2001. *Value, Respect, and Attachment*. Cambridge: Cambridge University Press.

Reginster, Bernard. 2016. "Affirmation and Absurdity." *Philosophy and Phenomenological Research* 92, 785–91.

Rind, B., & Bordia, P. 1995. "Effect of Server's 'Thank You' and Personalization on Restaurant Tipping." *Journal of Applied Social Psychology* 25, 745–51.

Rosati, Connie S. 2013a. "The Makropulos Case Revisited: Reflections on Immortality and Agency." In *The Oxford Handbook of Philosophy of Death*, edited by Ben Bradley, Fred Feldman, & Jens Johansson (Oxford: Oxford University Press), 355–90.

Rosati, Connie S. 2013b. "The Story of a Life." *Social Philosophy & Policy* 30, 21–50.

Rosenbaum, Stephen E. 1993a. "Epicurus and Annihilation." In *The Metaphysics of Death*, edited by John Martin Fischer (Stanford, CA: Stanford University Press), 293–304.

Rosenbaum, Stephen E. 1993b. "How to Be Dead and Not Care: A Defense of Epicurus." In *The Metaphysics of Death*, edited by John Martin Fischer (Stanford, CA: Stanford University Press), 119–34.

Ruben, David-Hillel. 1988. "A Puzzle about Posthumous Predication." *The Philosophical Review* 97, 211–36.

Scarre, Geoffrey. 2007. *Death*. London: Routledge.

Scheffler, Samuel. 2013. *Death & the Afterlife*, edited by Niko Kolodny. Oxford: Oxford University Press.

Sen, Amartya. 1993. "Capability and Well-Being." In *The Quality of Life*, edited by Martha Nussbaum and Amartya Sen (Oxford: Clarendon Press), 30–53.

Sidgwick, Henry. 1890. *The Methods of Ethics*, 4th edition. London: Macmillan and Co.

Sigrist, Michael J. 2015. "Death and the Meaning of Life." *Philosophical Papers* 44, 83–102.

Silverstein, Harry. 1993. "The Evil of Death." In *The Metaphysics of Death*, edited by John Martin Fischer (Stanford, CA: Stanford University Press), 95–116.

Smilansky, Saul. 1997. "Should I Be Grateful to You for Not Harming Me?" *Philosophy and Phenomenological Research* 57, 585–97.

Smilansky, Saul. 2007. *Ten Moral Paradoxes*. Malden, MA: Blackwell.

Smilansky, Saul. 2012. "Life Is Good." *South African Journal of Philosophy* 31, 69–78.

Smilansky, Saul. 2013. "Morally, Should We Prefer Never to Have Existed?" *Australasian Journal of Philosophy* 91, 655–66.

Streng, Frederick J. 1989. "Gratitude and Thankful Joy in Indian Buddhism." In *Spoken and Unspoken Thanks: Some Comparative Soundings*, edited by John B. Carman & Frederick J. Streng (Cambridge, MA: Center for the Study of World Religions), 43–53.

Sullivan, Meghan. 2018. *Time Biases: A Theory of Rational Planning and Personal Persistence*. Oxford: Oxford University Press.

Teichman, Jenny. 1993. "Humanism and the Meaning of Life." *Ratio* 6, 155–64.

Temkin, Larry S. 2008. "Is Living Longer Better?" *Journal of Applied Philosophy* 25, 193–210.

Warren, James. 2004. *Facing Death: Epicurus and His Critics*. Oxford: Oxford University Press.

Walker, A. D. M. 1980–81. "Gratefulness and Gratitude." *Proceedings of the Aristotelian Society* 81, 39–55.

Wallace, R. Jay. 2013. *The View from Here: On Affirmation, Attachment, and the Limits of Regret*. Oxford: Oxford University Press.

Wallace, R. Jay. 2016. "Replies to Symposiasts on *The View from Here*." *Philosophy & Phenomenological Research* 92, 792–805.

Watkins, Philip C. 2004. "Gratitude and Subjective Well-Being." In *The Psychology of Gratitude*, edited by Robert A. Emmons & Michael E. McCullough (Oxford: Oxford University Press): 167–92.

Williams, Bernard. 1973. "The Makropulos Case: Reflections on the Tedium of Immortality." In *The Problems of the Self* (Cambridge: Cambridge University Press), 82–100.

Wittgenstein, Ludwig. 1961. *Tractatus Logico-Philosophicus*. Trans. David Pears and Brian McGuinness. London: Routledge.

Wolf, Aaron. 2018. "Reviving Concurrentism about Death." *Journal of Value Inquiry* 52: 179–85.

Wood, Alex M., Froh, Jeffrey J., & Geraghty, Adam W. A. 2010. "Gratitude and Well-Being: A Review and Theoretical Integration." *Clinical Psychology Review* 30, 890–905.

Woodward, James. 1986. "The Non-Identity Problem." *Ethics* 96, 804–34.

Yourgrau, Palle. 1993. "The Dead." In *The Metaphysics of Death*, edited by John Martin Fischer (Stanford, CA: Stanford University Press), 137–68.

Zhuangzi. 2009. *Zhuangzi: The Essential Writings with Selections from Traditional Commentaries*, trans. Brook Ziporyn (Indianapolis: Hackett).

INDEX

For the benefit of digital users, indexed terms that span two pages (e.g., 52–53) may, on occasion, appear on only one of those pages.